OUTPUT
THINKING

COPYRIGHT © 2023 John Seiffer

CREATIVE DIRECTOR: Saeah Wood

PRODUCTION AND EDITORIAL MANAGER: Amy Reed

EDITORIAL: Harriet Power, Amy Reed, Terri Armstrong Welch

DESIGN: Ivica Jandrijević

PRODUCTION & EDITORIAL ASSISTANT: Laura Tutko

Except as noted below, all figures are original creations of the Author and Publisher.

Grateful acknowledgment is made to the following for use of the New York and Erie Railroad diagram on page 28:

McCallum, D. C. , Cartographer, G. H. Henshaw, and Publisher New York and Erie Railroad Company. New York and Erie Railroad diagram representing a plan of organization: exhibiting the division of academic duties and showing the number and class of employees engaged in each department: from the returns of 1855. https://www. loc.gov/item/2017586274/.

PAPERBACK ISBN: 978-1-930417-00-7
E-BOOK ISBN: 978-1-930417-03-8

OUTPUT
THINKING

Scale Faster,
Manage Better,
Transform Your Company

JOHN SEIFFER

CONTENTS

CHAPTER 5. USES OF OUTPUT THINKING

CHAPTER 6. ASSIGNING OUTPUTS TO PEOPLE

CHAPTER 7. MANAGER OUTPUTS

CHAPTER 8. OUTPUTS COME FROM SYSTEMS

CHAPTER 9. HOW TO DOCUMENT YOUR SYSTEMS

CHAPTER 10. HOW SYSTEMS CHANGE AS YOUR COMPANY SCALES

CHAPTER 11. HOW TO DOCUMENT YOUR WHOLE COMPANY

CHAPTER 12. SYSTEMS INVENTORY, AKA THE SEVEN BUCKETS

CHAPTER 13. REMOVE YOURSELF FROM THE DAY-TO-DAY

CHAPTER 1

FEAR!

THAT WAS THE one-word title of an article in *Inc.* magazine about the worry, anxiety, and often sheer terror that plagues business owners. It got the most response of any article the magazine had ever run, because every business owner has felt that fear. Many business owners wake up terrified in the wee hours of the night. I know I have.

In 1991 I was living in Plano, Texas, and a friend had started a business renting movies from his video store to nearby apartment complexes. They'd take 50 movies for a month and would offer them overnight to their residents for free—it was a marketing tool for them. And each month he'd exchange the 50 movies for another 50.

We thought the business had more potential than his small video store could supply. So he and I partnered up to grow this thing as a company, separate from the video store. I would invest to buy the movies for each new apartment complex and track the data so accounts wouldn't get the same movies too often. He would do the selling. But it didn't go as planned (most start-ups don't) and we couldn't agree on how to move forward. Since he had no money to buy me out, I bought him out using most of my life's savings. I went home that night to my house (with a mortgage), my wife, and my two young boys. Several times I'd wake up in a cold sweat wondering if I'd made the biggest mistake of my life.

This story has a happy ending, though I know many don't. For one thing, I had a side gig. For years I'd had a window-cleaning company. It was reasonably successful and was paying the bills. I kept that company with a small crew going even as I worked a full-time contractor job in an office 40 hours a week, and later when I got involved in the video business. It turned out the video business just had a long sales cycle, and it eventually kicked into gear. It kicked in so well, I sold the window business and decided to move 1,500 miles from Texas to the Northeast where I'm from. Isn't business supposed to allow you to live the life you want? No offense to Texans, but I prefer four seasons.

My dilemma was that it didn't make sense to move the company. Most of our customers were in the South and Southwest, and Plano was an ideal location to serve them from. I remember thinking that there are plenty of companies with a headquarters in one state and a branch office in another. If they could do it, I was sure I'd be able to figure out how I could make it work. This was in the early nineties when the movies were on VHS and the internet was not what it is today. My team would have to overnight me data tapes to put into my computer so I could see what was going on.

As I got a handle on that business, I got a call from someone I used to work with. She suggested I look into something called coaching (it hadn't become a buzzword yet). I looked into it and really liked it. In 1994 I started coaching other business owners. This allowed me to get involved in two things I love: learning about how companies work and teaching what I learn. A group of us formed the International Coaching Federation or ICF (https:// coachingfederation.org) and I was their fourth president in 1998. That organization is still going, and in 2021 they had over 50,000 members worldwide.

I had structured the video business so it didn't demand too much of my time despite growing 30 or 40% a year, as it did for a while. That left me free to coach and to nurture the ICF, and learn how nonprofit organizations worked.

Do you see a pattern here? I ran a window-cleaning company on the side of a full-time contracting gig. Then when my video company was starting to take off, I moved halfway across the country. (My accountant joked that it grew so well after I left that maybe I should move to Russia.) While running that, I built a coaching practice and ran a nonprofit.

In other words, that's been my modus operandi—juggling multiple companies while none of them depend on me for the day-to-day activities. This is the kind of challenge I love. In addition to the fear I'd felt after buying out my partner, I've experienced the other extreme emotion that comes along with running a company: the exhilaration of loving what you do and making money from it.

Lots of others feel this exhilaration too. Often we're the same people who feel the terror. But if you want your business to run better, it doesn't matter if you're motivated by fear, exhilaration, or something else. It's not your motivations that are effective. It's your actions.

What I'm trying to put in this book are the lessons I've learned running my companies for over 40 years, as well as those I've learned from working with hundreds of clients across the US and Europe in 25 years of coaching. And through it all, I've learned a lot of things you should do and I've learned by experience many things you shouldn't do. I won't say I've cracked anything like the Da Vinci Code, but I have seen similarities across all industries. The main thing I've learned is:

DON'T BE LIKE LARRY!

LARRY'S COMPANY GREW AND HE MADE LESS MONEY

Larry had a framing company.[1] He and his crew would show up at a housing development to build the frames of the houses on top of the foundations someone else had poured. Then they'd move on to the next house so

---

[1] The stories in this book come from clients I've worked with, companies I've owned, or ones I've known about or studied. I've changed names and certain identifying aspects.

the electricians, plumbers, and other tradespeople could come in and do their work.

Larry was taking home about a thousand dollars a week with just one crew. This was a good living back in the seventies—about $250k a year in 2022 dollars—and Larry decided to expand. He hired a second crew and soon he was taking home $750 a week instead of $1,000. Well, that wasn't quite working. So he expanded again, and pretty soon he had three crews and was taking home only $500 a week.

Why did his profit decrease? And why was his experience, when stepping away from the crew, so different from mine—even though he hadn't moved halfway across the country like I did?

Were his people lazy when the boss was away? Did he hire people who didn't know what they were doing? Were they not incentivized properly? None of these were the problem. But these questions all have one thing in common. They focus on the people, not the outputs those people produce.

It's actually pretty common for owners of small companies to see their businesses get into trouble when they step away from the day-to-day operations. And the assumption is it has to do with the employees. But usually that's not the reason.

You see, when Larry was on-site with his one crew he was producing a certain output without even realizing it. And when he left the crew on its own, he didn't replace that output. As a result, the crews couldn't operate efficiently. The crucial output he was producing wasn't the frames he was building, rather it was an efficient and well-functioning crew that built the frames.

He was performing the role of a supervisor, often called a crew lead, a team leader, or in Larry's case, a foreman (because in the seventies the construction industry was primarily men). And the output of a team leader is the improved performance of their team. Good team leaders produce this output not by berating people and pushing them to work harder. They do it by being responsible for things like scheduling, ordering supplies, quality checks, and prioritizing who does what when. And they do it by protecting the team from unnecessary meetings and interruptions. In other words, they help their teams do better work. All of this made Larry's team more efficient and effective at building frames.

But nobody did this when Larry wasn't there. This is a common trap of running a company: it can't seem to function without you. I've known business owners who go years without a vacation. Some don't even take days off. But back to Larry. When he pulled away from his crew, he left a gap—the outputs he'd been producing as a team leader. And he didn't replace himself as a team leader because he thought having good people was enough. It's true that having good people is important, but building a strong business takes something else as well. Especially if you want that business to be able to do well when you're not in the field with the crews.

If Larry had been aware of the gap he was leaving when the crew was on its own, it would have been a simple fix to train someone and authorize them to function as the supervisor and keep the crews working effectively. He'd need one for each crew. But seeing his company as a collection of people, he assumed if he got good people who knew how to build frames, that's all he'd need.

Larry's situation isn't unique: too many owners feel trapped in their companies. The day-to-day work can't happen without them being directly involved. This limits their ability to grow the company or even take a day off. This is a very common problem among company owners. And it stems from a misunderstanding of the role good people play in a company.

Unlike Larry, when I stepped away from the day-to-day work in my companies, I was aware of the results I was producing and I made sure that someone else would make them happen. That allowed me to focus on growing the company and freed me up to make some of the life choices owning a business should provide.

This takes a different mindset from the idea that all you need is good people. This new mindset is what I call Output Thinking. That's what this book is all about. My goal is to help you to systemize your company, scale fast, and remove yourself from the day-to-day routine as your company grows. It takes Output Thinking to do that.

HOW TO USE THIS BOOK

This book is written for business owners and CEOs of SMBs (small to medium businesses). These are companies with 5 to 250 employees and $1m to $25m in revenue. There's no hard-and-fast definition of an SMB, but that's the range of companies I've worked with. They are privately held, some are owned entirely by the person or people who run them, and some have outside investors (silent partners). They are generally run to make a profit over the long term, not to be flipped for sale. These are bigger than "lifestyle businesses" but boy oh boy, do they provide a great lifestyle. They provide money, even wealth, plus the option to do the kind of work you enjoy, the ability to hire people you want to work with, and the opportunity to live where you want.

Unfortunately, these dreams are not a reality for many SMB owners. Too many feel their life is serving their company rather than the other way around. But when the company is serving you, you can work remotely like Richard, who owns a company in Southern California that makes automobile parts while he lives in Northern California closer to the wineries from where he stocks his extensive wine cellar. Or like Lori and her husband Troy, who had a small chain of retail stores in LA and decided to open two more in Atlanta. They have houses in both places and commute when they aren't busy with other things (he's an artist and she's an actress).

Or you can stay on-site like Dan, who wanted to double the size of the company his dad had started 50 years before he took over. Or you can be like Josh, who hired me because his company had been bought by a global enterprise and he wanted to make sure he got his earnout. They both accomplished their goals.

How much you work, where you work, what you do: that's up to you if you use Output Thinking to systemize your company. My hope is that learning the concepts in this book will allow you to make the life choices you want to make. As I said, the book is geared toward owners of SMBs who have almost complete control over their companies. However, if you run a different kind of organization, a nonprofit, or manage a team at a large firm, I think you'll find some value here too.

Here's how the different parts of the book can help.

Output Thinking is viewing your company through the lens of the outputs people produce. In chapters 2 through 6, we'll see why this is such a big change from how most people view their businesses, and how it can allow you to grow your company faster and manage people better.

Two important aspects of Output Thinking are the outputs expected from managers and the outputs expected from a CEO. We'll cover those in chapter 7. Understanding these is how you get away from doing the day-to-day work, if you want to. You don't have to physically distance yourself from your company like I did. But not being tied to the day-to-day functioning of your business allows you to focus on more strategic activities, grow your company faster, or acquire other companies if that's what you want.

Systems are a way to replicate and scale the production of outputs. Many companies—even successful ones—are run by very intuitive people. What they do comes naturally to them. I equate them to chefs (or grandmothers) who make great food without following a recipe. Dinner is delicious, but you can't build a company on that kind of expertise. In chapters 8 through 11 we'll see how systems allow you to get the wisdom, experience, and intuition out of people's heads and diffuse it throughout your company.

Buckets are a way to group all the outputs every business needs so you can think about your company structure in a better way. I admit it's kind of a goofy word to use in this context, but I use it because it's different from words like "departments" or "teams," and different words allow us to see things differently. This process comes from an exercise I do with clients called a Systems Inventory. In chapters 12 and 13 you'll get a modified version of this inventory that you can apply to your company.

Exercises. There's a science and an art to running a company. The science is the stuff that's (nearly) always true. The art is how you adapt the science and apply it to your situation. Throughout the book I'll be sharing ways you can put these insights to work in your organization. I call them CEO Time activities. They are some specific ways you can work **on** your business rather than **in** it. Here are your first two:

👉 Grab some CEO TIME

Block out a weekly appointment on your calendar with the most important CEO you know—that's you! You'll use this time to work on your business. That means doing those things that are important but not urgent. Here are the rules.

1. Schedule it weekly. I recommend two hours minimum. Same time every week.

2. Find a special location. Don't do it where you normally work. Find a different room in your house, a coffee shop, a library, or somewhere else you enjoy.

3. No interruptions! No email, no phone. Tell everyone not to interrupt you unless there's fire or blood.

TWO HOURS A WEEK?!? I hear you saying. Where am I going to find that? The truth is you can't *find* CEO Time—you have to *grab* it. Because it's not urgent, there will never be an opening in your schedule for it unless you make one and protect it. Put it in your calendar as a weekly appointment and guard it zealously. If you don't do this, you're letting others control your schedule.

👉 Get a CEO Notebook

If you like writing on paper, get a fancy notebook and pen. If your handwriting is as bad as mine, find something electronic you enjoy using. Maybe a new tablet, a special app, or just a particular file you'll use only for this. I use OneNote, but do what works for you. There's only one rule for the notebook:

1. Date each entry whenever you write one. It will make the notebook so much more useful.

What do you do in your CEO Time? You think! And capture your thoughts about the business in your CEO Notebook.

You can also use it for some of the other exercises you read here (and other places). In general, you're looking for ways to improve the business, and ways to prevent problems—not just solve them. You'll think about strategic relationships you want to develop or processes you want to improve. Stuff like that—things that are important but not urgent.

Of course, you'll probably also discover some urgent things you need to do. So move them to your calendar or whatever tool you use for your to dos at the end of your CEO Time.

You'll uncover some great ideas (and lots that are not so great). Capture them all. Putting them in your CEO Notebook allows you to get them out of your head, so you don't lose them but won't have to focus on them immediately.

If you want more ways to structure your thinking, I've got a list of potential pages for your CEO Notebook. They're in Word format so you can print or copy as you see fit. You can download them at this link: https://decipherpublications.com/output-thinking-extras/.

There's something John D. Rockefeller said that I think provides some good insight into how to build a company. (I hesitate to identify too closely with many of the things Rockefeller did to build his company, but I think this one can be useful.)

> Has anyone given you the law of the offices? No? It is this: nobody does anything if he can get anybody else to do it. … As soon as you can, get someone whom you can rely on, train him in the work, sit down, cock up your heels and think out some way for the Standard Oil to make some money.
>
> **—JOHN D. ROCKEFELLER**[2]

When you've got your feet up thinking, that's CEO Time. As for training someone else on the work—that's what Output Thinking is all about. Let's get to it.

[2] Ron Chernow, Titan: The Life of John D. Rockefeller, Sr. (United States: Knopf Doubleday Publishing Group, 2007), 178.

CHAPTER 2

OUTPUT THINKING

YOUR BUSINESS IS NOT PEOPLE

Your business is made up of people. I'm sure this is a fact you're painfully aware of every payday. As your company grows, it will have even more people. Some of those people will manage other people. And some will manage those managers. As companies grow, we can't keep the relationships of all the people in our heads, so we typically plot those relationships on an org chart with boxes that have people's names and titles in them and, if the chart is really fancy, people's pictures. Then there are lines connecting various boxes to show who reports to whom, with dotted lines to show less formal reporting relationships.

But thinking of your company through the lens of an org chart hinders your ability to manage your people and grow your company. Let's start by asking why you hire people in the first place. You hire them to do something: to produce some kind of results, some output that will ultimately lead to profits. Thinking of your company through the lens of an org chart can cloud your view of the reasons you hired those people: the outputs you want them to produce. Focusing on the outputs is what I call Output Thinking.

You see, most people think of their companies as a collection of people who produce certain outputs. Instead, I'm going to suggest you think of your business as a collection of outputs that are produced by people. "Wait," I hear you saying. "You just moved the words around. How is that different?"

Let me tell you another story. This one is about how Output Thinking saved a company.

A CAR DEALERSHIP IS SAVED BY OUTPUT THINKING

When the economy crashed in 2008, there was a car dealership in Milford, Connecticut, which was in danger of going out of business if they didn't cut a significant number of staff. Just before the recession hit they had embarked on an expansion to their facility. Unfortunately, between the construction and the drop in sales, they didn't have the cash to keep everyone on the payroll until the economy came back.

Obviously it was a very emotional process to figure out who should stay and who would have to go. But the difficulty was compounded because they were thinking about it wrong. Like owners of most small companies, their conception of the company was centered around people: Joe does this, Nadia does that. Add that to the emotional connections with the people who worked there and their years of loyalty, and the top leaders were paralyzed, even knowing that if they did nothing it was likely that everyone would lose their jobs.

What allowed them to move forward with this unpleasant task was thinking of their company as a collection of outputs, not people. Here's how they did it. They made a conservative projection of what sales would be over the next few years. Then they took out a blank sheet of paper and mapped out which outputs would be required to generate those sales and serve the now diminished customer base. With the outputs defined, they could start assigning people to produce them, based on each individual's skills, training, and capacity. That let them see who they needed to keep and who would have to be let go. This didn't make the task less horrible, but it gave them a way to do it and allow the company to survive.

Output Thinking isn't just semantics. It's a different way of focusing on what needs to be produced to keep your company functioning and profitable.

OUTPUTS ARE MORE PERMANENT THAN PEOPLE

The main reason Output Thinking is so powerful is that for your company to survive, it needs pretty much the same outputs all the time. But people will move around. They move up, or down, or out, or into your organization. Don't get me wrong, your company needs people. It's just that no individual is irreplaceable (or shouldn't be), otherwise you'd never be able to promote anyone. And if you're irreplaceable as the owner, you'll be stuck doing the same thing every day—owning a job not a company, as the saying goes.

Outputs, on the other hand, are irreplaceable. If nobody produces them, the business falls apart. People move, but the outputs remain constant. Let me give you an obvious example. Suppose an employee goes on parental leave for a significant period of time. You don't just ignore the outputs they were producing, you reassign them. Even if an employee is out for a day, some outputs are so critical they can't wait and need to be done that day regardless of who's doing them.

THE PROBLEM WITH JOB TITLES

People often assume the job title indicates what that person produces. This leads to org chart thinking—very different from Output Thinking. Job titles have a purpose, but it's not what you think. We'll get to that in a minute. For now, I want to show you some of the reasons org chart thinking is limiting.

Job titles are not consistent

The same title in different companies will be responsible for vastly different outputs. There might be someone with the title Marketing Director in one company. The output they produce is a strategic marketing plan, and they oversee a team to implement that plan. They don't make any of the collateral material or social media posts. But in another company, the person with the title of Marketing Director is the one who makes the brochures and posts to social media.

Titles can even be used differently in the same company. How sure are you that everyone with the title "Senior Engineer" is responsible for producing similar outputs?

Job titles can limit people

People may have more specific strengths than are covered in their job title or role. Suppose we have a receptionist (let's call him Bill). Bill's main job is to handle the incoming phone calls, as well as visitors who walk in, and emails that show up in a general email box. Then Bill either responds directly to these questions and requests or routes them to the proper person. Those are good outputs for that job title. However, Bill might also be great at fixing the printer when it disconnects from the network and rebooting the router when it needs it. Those are outputs that have nothing to do with the role of "Receptionist." They are, in fact, outputs that are usually associated with the title of Tech Support.

In a small company those outputs are attached to the person, not the role. And they are important to the functioning of the company. If you don't recognize them properly, then Bill might not have the time to do them well. When you want to promote Bill, the fact that he produces those outputs may get lost until the printer crashes again. Or worse, Bill might get a poor review of his performance because he's taking time away from being a receptionist to keep the network running—an output that's critical but not reflected in his job title.

Job titles can be misused to "reward" a person

When I say "misused" I mean not useful at best and very problematic at worst. Here's an example of the best case.

One day I walked into the office of my client, Dan. He runs an advanced manufacturing company with about 65 employees. They make intricate parts out of metal for very specialized uses. They have parts in submarines, they repair airplane parts, and have even made parts that are now on at least two of the Mars rovers.

On this day he said to me, "I just promoted my general manager to a vice president." In over five decades the company had never had a VP before. "Why?" I asked. The answer, it turned out, was that the GM was in his late fifties and had been a loyal employee with the company for many years. Dan wanted to keep him around until his retirement, and Dan thought this would be a nice way to encourage that.

The next question I asked was, "What will he do on his first day as VP that's different from what he did on his last day as GM?" Dan was silent. So basically, he had given this person a raise and a new title, but not expected any different output from him. In truth there wasn't a need to—all the outputs were already being produced properly. I'm all for raises and promotions but in my view they should be earned, not given retroactively. There are other ways to reward loyalty. In this case, the promotion was not problematic. Both Dan and the VP continued to

produce the needed outputs and the company continued to grow. In fact, the revenue doubled in a few years.

But sometimes, rewarding someone with a job title can
be a real problem. Jennifer was doing a great job as a construction manager but wanted to use those skills to start
her own company as the on-site eyes and ears of develop-
ers, making sure the general contractor is doing their job
properly. She landed a couple of small customers but didn't
really know how to grow a company. By the time I started
working with her, one of her first employees, Thomas, had
convinced her that the company had even more potential
than she knew. Turns out he was right.

Jennifer promoted Thomas to Project Executive on
their biggest project to date. She was happy to give him
that title because he had been inspirational in helping
her see how big the company could be. She was excited
for him to help grow the company. In her mind, the title
meant he would manage the others on the project and
be responsible for its successful completion.

She had assumptions about what outputs a project executive ought to produce. She assumed that Thomas was
the guy to produce the right outputs without ever specifying what they were. And because the company was
young and she couldn't pay him as much as she hoped
he was worth, Jennifer assumed the title would encourage loyalty.

However, Thomas was only good at certain parts of
his job. He did well with some on-site activities but he
was not good at delegating or managing others. And he
didn't take charge of the relationship with the developer
they were working for, so he relied too heavily on Jennifer

for advice. This kept her from doing some of the things she needed to do.

The problem was not exactly Thomas's limited ability. There was a place for the things he did well in the organization. However, that place was not as a project executive.

When Jennifer hired me, we started to look at the outputs required to do a good job managing a project, rather than job titles. We listed the outputs independent of the job titles, because every job of every size needed them all to be done. However, when a job became big enough that there was too much work for one person, those outputs could be grouped by skill (and hence salary) and doled out to one or more project engineers, a project manager (who also managed the engineers), and a project executive who often could oversee more than one project. Thomas's outputs were more in line with those typically produced by a project engineer.

The problem for Jennifer and Thomas was that because he had been given an inflated title before the outputs were defined, he was in over his head and now they were faced with an unpleasant situation. His title and his salary didn't accurately reflect the outputs he was producing. Thomas ended up leaving the company and Jennifer ended up hiring better people for more well-defined roles. But this problem could have been avoided had the outputs been specified early on.

This type of job title inflation is not uncommon in smaller, younger companies, where people are rewarded for their loyalty or for being part of a team when market-rate salaries are not always available. However, it usually causes problems as the company grows.

In larger companies, the "Peter Principle" comes into play. I'll have more to say about this later when we talk about the output needed from people who manage other people.

☛ CEO TIME: Job titles

Here are some ways to explore how job titles may be used (or misused) in your company.

1. Pick two people with the same job title. Write down the outputs they each produce. How different are the lists of outputs produced by the same job title?

2. Think of someone who's up for a promotion. Have you and they agreed on the outputs they'll be required to produce in their new position? Has anyone considered who will produce the outputs of their old position?

I'm not saying job titles are completely useless. One thing they do well is to function as signaling devices. When meeting with someone outside your company, your job title signals where you stand in the company. This is one reason some owners don't list "Owner" or "CEO" as their title. It can be useful in negotiations not to be known as the person with final authority.

Inside your company, titles can be more problematic. Job titles or roles can become a shortcut way of grouping outputs. You'll assume everyone with the title "Accounts Payable Clerk" is responsible for the same list of outputs. But this doesn't allow you the flexibility to tailor work to each person's unique mix of strengths and skills.

Titles are also powerful signaling devices inside your company. They show where people stand in relation to their colleagues. This is hard to do well, because you have to be consistent so that folks with the same title are expected to produce similar outputs, require similar training, and receive similar salaries.

There are a few large companies that don't use job titles. The W.L. Gore Company is a privately held company that manufactures Gore-Tex (among many other things). In 1985 they had a supreme commander and it wasn't the boss, according to this story from the *Chicago Tribune*.[3]

> Bill and Vieve Gore, founders of W.L. Gore & Associates, the $250 million [in 1985–$4.5 billion in 2022] maker of the Gore-Tex breathing synthetic fabric, have no patience whatsoever with titles. Other than those required by law, there are no official titles in the company—starting with Bill himself. Some time ago, Bill was in Flagstaff, Ariz., visiting one of Gore's 28 facilities. Walking the line, he ran into Sarah Clifton, a long-time employee.
>
> Sarah explained that she had been asked to attend a local meeting to talk about the company's unusual lack of structure. Her prospective hosts wanted her to explain "what I am." Bill replied, "Sarah, what do you want to be?" She had no ready answer, so he made a suggestion: "Why not 'Supreme Commander'?" Soon Sarah had formal calling cards printed: "Sarah Clifton, Supreme Commander." And why not?

IT'S EASIER TO MANAGE BY OUTPUTS THAN TITLES

I think the Gores have hit on something here. If you don't have job titles, how do you manage people? You manage by delineating the outputs each person is expected to produce. Job titles are assumed to be a shortcut way of grouping several outputs together. But this is usually counterproductive because listing individual outputs is more detailed than a job title and the same grouping is not always best for each person.

Many companies have tried what's called a matrix organization. That's where people have multiple bosses and they report to one boss for some things and a different boss for other things. This might be useful when each boss has different abilities and ways to support the different aspects of the work the employee does.

The problem with matrix management has always been that it's hard for people to have more than one boss inside a company. But freelance workers who work for several clients at once have more than one boss all the time. Due to the scope of work for each client, it's very clear what they need to do for each one. Scope of work in my view is just a description of outputs – and something that should be done with employees. Then different outputs could be managed by the person who's in the best position to manage that work.

☞ CEO TIME: How useful are job titles in your company?

Consider the job titles that exist in your company. Here are some questions to think about.

- What signals do job titles send to vendors, customers, and others outside your company?
- What signals do they send to people inside the company?
- Are they used consistently?
- Do they inspire people to do better work or just look for a promotion because of their status?
- Has there ever been a situation where you felt the title and the person's outputs were mismatched?

Before we leave this topic, I have to tell you the story of a business owner who did put "Owner" on his business card. William started a printing company with his wife, Heather. He had humorous business cards printed for everyone. Heather's said "Director of Euphoria" and William's said "President/Janitor." I'm sure that was accurate in the early days.

A few years later, I ran into William and his business card said "Owner/Janitor." I asked him what happened to the president and he said, "I got tired of talking to everyone so when we hit about 35 employees I made someone else president. Now everyone talks to him and he's the one who talks to me." I doubt that William does janitorial duties anymore.

THE PROBLEM WITH ORG CHARTS

Org charts show hierarchy in a company. This is their strength and their weakness. Sure, they show you who reports to whom and (theoretically) that a person is responsible for managing the people "underneath" them. There's some benefit to that. However, the org chart has two downsides.

1. It's upside down. As we'll see, part of a manager's job is to help their people do better work. That speaks to the concept of a servant leader. You'd never see that by looking at an org chart where the person with the most authority is at the top.

2. Many companies find a single hierarchy too limiting. That's why people have developed functional organizations, matrix organizations, and horizontal or flat organizations. In some companies, people have more than one boss. It's hard to show these relationships on an org chart.

Even the very first org chart that we know of was a hybrid. In 1855, Daniel McCallum and George Holt Henshaw made this diagram for the New York and Erie Railroad. If you look closely you'll see that it is a combination of hierarchical chains of command as well as a representation of the different railroad lines the company managed. It certainly is a beauty.

The biggest problem I have with org chart thinking is that it puts the focus on the wrong things. It encourages us to focus on people's jobs and the work they do, rather than the results or outputs they produce. You can see

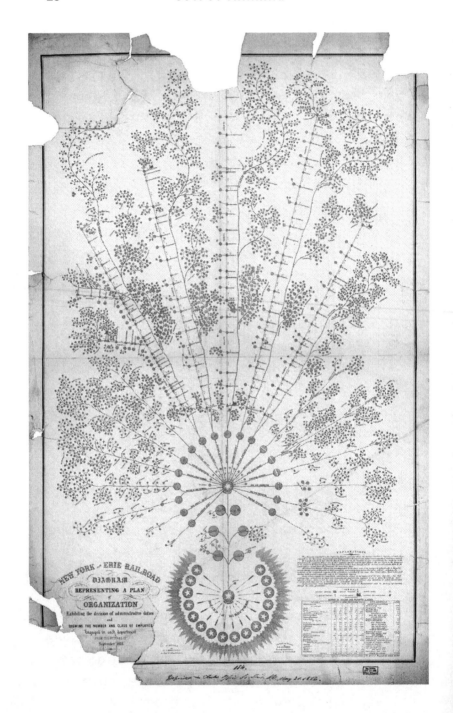

this in the language we use. We say someone is *"responsible* for XZY" rather than someone "will *produce* XYZ." But activity is not the goal: accomplishment is. This may seem a rather nerdy insight, but I think it's powerful. Changing what you say is the first step to changing what people hear and how they think. In order to get beyond org chart thinking, we have to look deeper into outputs. The way I use the term might be broader and more powerful than you expect.

CHAPTER 3

WHAT IS AN OUTPUT?

THERE'S A CHILD'S fairy tale about a shoemaker who cut his leather into pieces and left them on his table to make into finished shoes in the morning. While he was sleeping, the magic elves came in and finished up all his shoes. I guess it was the slow season at Santa's workshop. As soon as the shoes were finished, the elves disappeared. In the morning, the shoemaker woke up and the elves were gone, but he knew they'd been there. How did he know? He saw finished shoes where before there had been only pieces of leather piled on the table.

So if your people were elves, and they did their job in the middle of the night, how would you know what they'd done when you came to work in the morning? If you can describe that, you've described the output you expect from someone performing the function of "shoemaker" or whatever.

An output is something visible: an outcome, a deliverable, an obvious behavior; something produced after doing some work. It could be something physical, like a marketing brochure or a hamburger. It could also be a change in status—if your job is to clean a room, then a clean room is the output. It can even be something intangible like a relationship or a decision. But it is demonstrable and discernible. If you've ever defined the scope of work for a contractor, you've described the results you're willing to pay for. That's what I'm calling output.

SIX KINDS OF OUTPUTS

Before we get too far down this path, I want to talk about semantics. Consultants are famous for using normal words in slightly specific ways and charging people lots of money for it. I'm more interested in you understanding a concept than in what you call it.

For example, if you do a Google search for "outputs vs outcomes" you'll find a number of writings about the distinction (which I think is a distinction without a difference). BMC's article on it says an outcome is what the company needs to achieve, while outputs are the actions that contribute to achieving that outcome.[4] They say that if a bakery makes a Spiderman cake for a kid's birthday party, the cake is the output but happy kids are the outcome.

To me, the relevant distinction here is that there are some things you can control (the quality of the cake)

---

[4] https://www.bmc.com/blogs/outcomes-vs-outputs/

and some you can't (how people react to it). Your job as a business owner is to learn as much as you can about how people will react (knowing you'll never be able to predict it 100%), then use that insight to determine what your people can control and do your best to make the two line up. I don't think the labels are critical if you understand the concepts. I may even use "output" and "outcome" interchangeably along with "results" and "deliverables." I hope that doesn't bother you.

What I hope you see here is that looking at a company as a collection of outputs is fundamentally different from looking at that same company as an org chart of people, regardless of whether we call them outputs, outcomes, or results. So, with that said, here are six different kinds of outputs.

An output can be a thing

The elves produced shoes, for example. A salesperson's output is signed contracts.

An output can be a change in status

A janitor makes a room clean: that's their output. They don't make the rooms, but they make them clean. An inspector's output is approved parts that can go into inventory. Again, they don't make the parts, but they change the status to approved or rejected.

Outputs can be behavioral, but don't mistake them for attitudes

Sometimes output describes a behavior rather than a physical item. When that's the case, be sure to define what exact behaviors you want to see, not just what "attitude" you're looking for. Here's what I mean.

It's common to hear employees described as having a good attitude (or a bad one). People will say someone is a "team player," or they really "get it." This is not Output Thinking. It's a mental shortcut we humans tend to use to communicate a number of behaviors. But these words can mean different things to different people. What behaviors does a team player do that someone who is not a team player doesn't do?

You'll see this when a company does a values exercise to name the values they view as important, but doesn't describe how to make those values visible. People usually leave these exercises thinking, "I wonder how much that exercise cost the company?" It's not bad to define values. Getting a company's culture right can be very powerful. But it's more useful to describe visible behaviors you want in your culture than to use words like attitudes or values.

Bretton Putter of CultureGene.ai does a lot of work helping companies define their values. This is particularly useful for companies with remote workers who can't communicate their culture the way companies can when everyone's physically together. One of his exercises is to have each person take the words in a company's list of values and write what it means to them and how they see it in action.

Pause for a moment and imagine that "honesty" was one of your company values. Get out your CEO Notebook and jot down how you'd see it in action.

.

.

.

I'll wait.

.

.

.

OK. Done?

Here's what some people wrote. See how close it comes to what you wrote.

Honesty means ...

• We are known for candor and directness.

• We give considered and constructive feedback.

• We are quick to admit mistakes.

• We never talk behind another person's back.

It's not that these expressions of honesty are better or worse than yours. I have reservations about some of them myself. The point is that they are expressed in a more visible way than just the word "honesty." If you want people to live the values of your company culture, you have to describe them in visible, behavioral ways that everyone can agree on.

Let me give you another example. I recently had to take several flights with an injured leg that I could not put any weight on. So I was using a contraption called an iWALK (which I highly recommend). As a result, I was interacting with a number of flight attendants on the different flights and I noticed that I felt some of them were friendly and some of them were grumpy. But those are attitudes. So I started to think about what behaviors led me to those judgments. Here's what I came up with: eye contact (or lack of it), smiles not frowns, proactively asking if they could help me rather than waiting to be asked. Things like that are behaviors that are visible. It's tempting to say some of those people cared more—but honestly, I don't know what they felt. I just know what they did.

Outputs can be decisions

People in companies make decisions all the time. Some of those decisions are one-offs. Some are made over and over again. Someone is charged with making these decisions and they are part of that person's output. Here are some examples of repetitive decisions.

- **Extending credit.** Many companies need to decide whether they should sell to customers on credit or demand cash on delivery (COD). If they give the customer credit, they need to decide how much. These are examples of decisions that are made repeatedly. It's an output that's required if a sale is to go forward. You'd want to know who's responsible for producing that output so they can be trained and their decisions tracked and improved.

- **Hiring and firing.** Often there are guidelines from the human resources department (HR) to ensure these decisions are made in compliance with laws and regulations, but the decisions still have to be made by someone.

• **Strategy decisions** are made by the top-level management of a company. These are decisions about which markets to go into and which products to carry.

Every decision needs to be made by someone and, like any output, the person in charge of making a decision may change as you promote people and your company grows. But the decision must be made no matter who makes it. That's why it's useful to specify certain types of decisions as outputs. Then they can be assigned to people and those people can be trained and evaluated. Don't view decision-making as an innate skill of the individual. See it as an output that people can be trained to do better.

One advantage of this approach is that decisions can be made by people lower down in the organization once they are trained properly. This means people at the top will be interrupted less because the way they make decisions can be replicated. If you think this is impossible, consider that some of the best companies in the hospitality industry routinely train entry-level desk clerks and food servers to make decisions on the fly that result in great service.

Solving problems is an output

As someone moves up through the ranks of a company, it's common that their promotion is due to their ability and responsibility to solve different levels of problems. You would think solving problems is always a good thing. But whether it's good or not can depend on who does it. Let me give you an example of where it's not.

Companies who do a lot of tech support often have different levels of support. Level 1 people can solve the problems that are most common and the simplest. If they can't solve a problem, they'll elevate it to a level 2 person and so on.

Companies do this because level 3 people are more expensive and harder to recruit than level 2 people, who are more expensive than level 1 people. If the level 3 people spent their time telling us to reboot our computers, it would be wasteful. So you don't just want anyone spending time solving any and all problems. You want problems solved by the right people who can do it most effectively. This links to the concept of everyone playing at the top of their game—something we'll cover a little later.

Parceling out problems requires a process known in the medical world as triage: assessing the urgency of the problem and matching it with the person who can best solve it. Good triage is an output in its own right. If the system of triage and allocation of problems is not done well, it can be annoying to your customers. But that's a different issue from who actually solves the problems.

By thinking of problem-solving as an output, you can assign problems to people with the proper skills and training.

Relationships can be an output

Business development people are expected to cultivate relationships with potential customers or joint venture partners. Those are the outputs they are expected to produce. Relationships are also key outputs for business owners. They often have relationships with important suppliers or long-standing customers. This becomes important when an owner is exiting the company. Those relationships need to be transferred to someone else in the company or there will be problems for the new owner.

But it's not just the owner. If you consider that people will move in and out of your company, you want all of their business relationships to stay with the company. This should be considered when you decide if employees will be able to use their own laptops, cell phones, and emails when doing business.

TIPS FOR DEFINING OUTPUTS

Defining an output can be a little tricky—especially with knowledge workers. You might think some of the things I'm calling outputs are the work people do, and you wouldn't be wrong. But there's more to it than that. The work is what they do to produce the output; the output is the reason for the work. If you want to grow your company, it's important to describe the outputs separately from the work. Otherwise you won't be able to improve the systems and scale the company.

If you're having trouble describing an output, here are some things to try.

1. Consider the elves. If one of your employees did their work in the middle of the night and went home before you arrived, how would you know that they did a good job? What would you see? That's the output you want from them.

2. If you could only hire contractors, not employees, how would you define the scope of work for the contracts? Scope of work should focus on what they are expected to produce. Why not do that for employees?

3. If you had to run your company from a desert island with no internet, what would you need to see in a weekly message in the bottle that floated in from the company to know the company was on track? Those are likely the outputs you'd want to know about.

4. Imagine two people in the same role producing similar outputs. One does a decent job and one does a great job. What do you notice about the difference? How would you explain the difference to someone who didn't know the two people?

5. Pick an employee. Imagine they were out on extended leave. Make a list of the things you'd have to get someone else to do to fill the gap they left. That's a list of the outputs they produce. You'll likely find that only some of them are directly related to their role or job description. Discuss that list with the person and see what they can add to it.

☞ CEO TIME: List the outputs

Pick one of your direct reports. Use one or more of the techniques above to list all the outputs you expect from them. Be as specific as possible (as if they were an elf).

Then check with them and see if they agree with your list. Maybe they didn't realize you expected certain outputs from them. Maybe they produce outputs that you didn't realize they spend time on.

This may lead to you and them reprioritizing what they work on.

If you've done this well, what you'll have is the basis for their performance review in a format that will be obvious to both of you.

CHAPTER 4

PROPERTIES OF OUTPUTS

WHEN YOU DESCRIBE outputs, it's often useful to describe the properties you associate with them. In the story of the shoemaker, the elves didn't just make his shoes—they made such high-quality shoes he was able to sell them for twice his normal price and really grow his business. Makes you wish those elves were still in the labor force.

Here are some attributes to assign to outputs. My guess is you already have some assumptions about these qualities. To get the most from Output Thinking, it's useful to get your assumptions out of your head and down in writing.

NUMBERS

It's great if the output includes a number: 12 clean rooms per shift for a janitor, for example, or seven pairs of shoes for an elf. Some things you want to measure by the hour, some by the shift, some by the month. Pick the right time frame for numeric output.

CAPACITY

Going back to the janitorial example, what's the maximum number of rooms you would expect a janitor to clean in a given shift? Adding this to your description of the output allows you to do a couple of things. First, it shows you who is producing more and who might be producing fewer clean rooms. This is very useful for performance reviews and to see who might need more training or better equipment to improve their output.

Another thing that capacity allows you to do is see when you need to hire another person. Suppose the capacity of the typical janitor is 11 rooms per shift, then you get a new contract that adds 30 rooms. You'll see that you need to hire three new janitors. If you only hire 2, they'll be overwhelmed and the quality is likely to diminish. Which brings us to another attribute that's useful in some situations.

QUALITY

This is how you define a job well done. It's often used as an opposing metric to numerical output. By that I mean a janitor could produce more clean rooms if they don't clean them well—or they can clean them to such a degree that they don't have time to clean as many as you expect.

As a manager, it's your job to define the appropriate level of quality and any other characteristics of the outputs that are important.

TRAINING AND CERTIFICATIONS

Almost all outputs require some training to be able to produce them well. Some also require certifications by a third party, which may need to be renewed periodically. When you document your systems (which we'll cover in chapter 9), you can indicate what training or certification is required to produce a certain output. You can even provide a link to the training videos or documents. You might want to insert a date into your documentation to show when the certification needs to be renewed.

FREQUENCY

Many outputs are initiated or triggered by a specific date or time. For example, payroll is done on a certain day. Others are initiated by something else. And some outputs need to be done on a regular basis but not exactly tied to a date. For example, equipment maintenance is often scheduled by the hours a machine has been run. Other things need to be done quarterly, although the exact date is not critical.

We'll get more into what kicks off an output when we talk about systems in chapter 8. I've found that if the frequency is not properly taken into account, then the need for the output becomes urgent and other outputs must be delayed until they too become urgent. It's better to account for frequency as a property of the output itself and make sure that it gets scheduled properly.

If you want to remove yourself from the day-to-day routine, you must consider the frequency of the outputs you're responsible for. If something needs to be done daily or weekly, and you're the one to do it, then the business will suffer if you don't make time to produce those outputs. This often causes conflict with an owner who wants to work on more strategic aspects of the business because these aspects, while not often urgent, can require periods of intense involvement. For example, if you're consummating an important deal, you don't want to be distracted by having to generate a weekly schedule to keep your employees busy.

COST

Every output costs something to produce. This is essential to the unit economics of your business. Sometimes it's useful to add the cost into the output description to make sure your pricing is appropriate.

Those are some examples of attributes you might assign to your outputs. Some you'll just use temporarily for a specific project. Cost is an example of this. Costs change relatively often, so you might need it as part of your output description when you're figuring out your pricing, but you don't want to keep it there forever lest it get out of date.

EXAMPLE OF OUTPUTS IN A JANITORIAL COMPANY

Let's put together a fictitious janitorial company. The janitors clean the rooms of our customers. Their output is clean rooms. Furthermore, we can define the quality that we expect: the trash is emptied, the carpet vacuumed, and the room dusted. It's perhaps also important to note what we don't expect: the windows cleaned or upholstery steam cleaned (that's another job). Then we can list an expectation of capacity: each building or floor would have an amount of rooms we expect a single person to finish in a single shift. This will give us some idea of how many people we need to hire as we take on new accounts.

Perhaps some accounts use specialized chemicals for cleaning certain parts of their buildings. Those need training so they are used properly. And we can specify that.

When we have a large enough crew, we might need a supervisor. Their outputs would be quality checks on the crew, covering for no-shows, keeping the crew supplied with materials and equipment, and so on. And a supervisor would have a capacity listed for their outputs: how many janitors they can oversee. The capacities here will help us see how many people we need to hire when we land a new account.

Most of those aspects of the outputs are more or less permanent. But periodically we want to make sure our pricing is appropriate. So we might add cost to the attributes of the outputs. This would consider the wages and benefits we pay our janitors and supervisors. It would also allow us to calculate the cost per room or square foot that we must pay. However, this attribute is not permanent. Wages tend to go up and (sometimes) productivity does as well. So this would be a temporary aspect of the output, but it would be useful for the times you want to make sure your pricing is on target.

CHAPTER 5

USES OF OUTPUT THINKING

NOW THAT YOU know what an output looks like, we'll look at some of the ways Output Thinking makes running your company easier and more effective.

OUTPUTS ARE THE KEY TO ACCOUNTABILITY

One popular SMB consulting approach recommends replacing your org chart with an accountability chart. That's great as far as it goes. But you can't hold people accountable without an agreement about what they'll be accountable for, and what they're accountable for is producing outputs. Sometimes this is numbers—accountable to produce 100 widgets a day. Sometimes it's quality— the defect percentage must improve every year. Sometimes it's something like employee morale as measured by attrition. (Notice that phrase "as measured by"? It can help you see how the outputs you're holding someone accountable for will be made obvious.)

Directors are accountable for the outputs of their divisions. Managers and department heads are accountable for the outputs of their teams. Individual contributors are accountable for their individual outputs. It's accountability all the way down. Sounds simple when it's said like that. But a culture of accountability is not as common as you'd think. It's simple but not easy, and incredibly powerful—even though it leads to hard conversations if the outputs are not adequate.

OUTPUT THINKING REDUCES FRUSTRATION

Almost every business owner I've worked with (including myself) has been frustrated by a disconnect between what managers expect and what their employees (even good ones) produce. Besides being frustrating, this disconnect is an impediment to growth.

There are two sides to this disconnect: how employees perform and what you expect. Much has been written about employees and how to manage their performance. But very little has addressed the expectation side of this frustration. And without clarity on what to expect, you can't do a good job of managing. The work I've done helping owners solve this problem is what gave rise to this approach I call Output Thinking. Here's what I've found.

- Some expectations are explicit but many are implicit. They are left unsaid and understood mostly through intuition. Intuition can be powerful, but it has its limits.

- Output Thinking helps to translate intuition into explicit expectations.

By properly describing all the outputs your company needs and then matching them with people's unique mix of skills and training, you can solve this disconnect, grow your company faster, and be a better manager. Not only will your people be more productive, they'll enjoy work more and be more engaged. This is because the vast majority of people really want to do a good job. But often they're hindered by not knowing all the details of what a good job looks like to their boss. Output Thinking solves this problem.

Assume and expect are red flags

Here's a tip. When you find yourself saying (or even thinking) things like:

- "I just assumed they would ..."
- "I'd just expect people to ..."
- "I shouldn't have to explain ..."

These are red flags that indicate there's a disconnect with an output that is required or expected. The best thing to do in this case is to make sure you're clear on the output you want to see and that you've communicated it in sufficient detail to the other person.

Here's a very common example. Often someone says of a lower-level employee, "I shouldn't have to tell someone to call if they're going to be late to work." You are 100% right. You shouldn't have to. But do you want to be right or be happy? If someone doesn't know to call (or doesn't do it) then apparently you do have to tell them how to function in your organization. I won't get into why they may not do this or know this—it doesn't matter. You should just be explicit about what you want them to do and help them do better.

OUTPUT THINKING IS THE ANTIDOTE TO MICROMANAGEMENT

Let's expand on the idea above that outputs need to be clearly communicated. I'll go so far as to say the most important part of a manager's job is defining the outputs an employee needs to produce to be successful. Managers should do this in very specific detail. Most people want to go home at the end of the day knowing they did a good job. The problem is it's often not obvious what a good job looks like. This is particularly true for knowledge work. The manager's job is to define a "good job" by clearly describing expected outputs.

This should be done in big ways, like the key performance indicators (KPIs) you expect them to hit each month and quarter. But it should also be done in small ways. Have you ever asked an employee to handle something in addition to their regular work? When you did, I bet you had an inkling of how long it should take and how soon you needed it done. Most people do. That timing is a critical piece of the output you need.

But many managers don't communicate that part of the output they expect to their employees. Instead, they say something like, "Can you please take care of this?"

And then they wait. If they haven't heard anything in a few days, they start to wonder if they should say something. They don't want to be seen as micromanaging.

Let's consider what micromanagement really is. I consider it to be telling someone how to do a job in ways that are seen as arbitrary and disrespectful. Sometimes they are seen that way because they are. Other times they are seen that way because of a lack of sufficient detail. Let's unpack this.

Often micromanagement means insisting on how something is done, not the output that needs to be produced. A lazy manager will combine the two when they should be separated. There's a lot of research to indicate that people are motivated by autonomy: the ability to control what they do. Daniel Pink has written a great book on this topic called *Drive: The Surprising Truth About What Motivates Us*. If you define outputs properly, you can give people as much autonomy as possible without compromising what needs to be accomplished. You'll often find that people come up with better ways to produce the outputs than you were aware of. When we talk about how to document systems, I'll show you how to capture those better ideas.

Sometimes an aspect of the output a person needs to produce can seem arbitrary. In cases like that, what appears to be micromanagement only seems that way because the person doesn't understand the whole process. There's a simple fix: explain the rest of the process to them. Or better yet, have the person they're handing their output off to explain their part of the work. It can sound like this: "I need this back by Wednesday so I can put it together with some other things and get a proposal to the client by Friday." Or you could say: "We need to get invoices out every Thursday by noon so some of our clients will pay by the following Friday. That brings in cash quicker so our cost of capital is lower and we can spend more money growing the company." That's not random or autocratic. But it can seem that way if those connections are not explained.

Of course if something is arbitrary, stop insisting on it. But many times, even when something seems arbitrary, there is a deeper reason behind the requirement, and one that ultimately affects how we serve customers.

Being disrespectful is the other part of micromanagement. Employees feel like their bosses dump things on them without taking into account what else is on their plate. But it's not the boss's responsibility to know everything an employee is doing at the moment. A better way to delegate is to say, "I need this done by Wednesday because of XYZ. How does that fit with what else you've got going?" Then make it safe for the employee to say, "Well, I'm busy with A, B & C. Which of those things do you want me to postpone?" And the two of you can agree on priorities.

OUTPUTS MAKE FOR GREAT MEETINGS

Meetings are a superpower if you do them right and hell if you do them wrong. Most meeting advice says to start with an agenda. I think an agenda should come second. First you should decide what you want the output of the meeting to be—*why* you're meeting in the first place. The agenda is a tool for how to get that outcome (and it may or may not be the best tool).

Some meetings can have more than one output. Here is a list of typical things that can be outputs of meetings.

- Ideas: use a brainstorming meeting.

- Decisions: use a meeting to arrive at a consensus decision *or* hear everyone's input before a leader makes a decision.

- Commitment to a plan: use a meeting to hear everyone's concerns and get buy-in.

- Bonding and camaraderie: in-person meetings are great for personal connection.

- Focus: daily huddles focus people on the work they'll accomplish that day. They also provide peer pressure, which is a different output but useful.

- Insight: regular one-on-one meetings are great for getting insight from your people.

- Communicating work status: many times, a meeting is a lazy way to communicate this. Twelve people are in the meeting and only three are affected by knowing the status of each other's work. As often as possible, work status should be communicated another way—such as through software—so you can use the meeting to produce another output.

When you consider the outputs you want from your meetings, you'll be able to see which ones would benefit from an agenda and craft one appropriately. For example, a daily huddle benefits from an agenda with very tight time constraints on each portion of the meeting. These are repeated in the same order every time. Then the output is a focus on the day's work and uncovering any potential problems that may need to be dealt with (in another meeting).

This degree of structure would be inappropriate for a meeting where you want to get commitment to a plan of action. If that's the output you're going for, you want to allow time for people's ideas and objections to be heard, and you can't tell ahead of time how long that will take. The ultimate outcome from this type of meeting is that the final plan is adopted; and even if not everyone agrees with it 100%, they can abide by the principle called "disagree and commit." This concept was pioneered by Andy Grove at Intel and later used by Jeff Bezos at Amazon.

OUTPUTS BECOME YOUR JOB DESCRIPTIONS

Most job descriptions are terrible because they completely ignore the reason you hire people. They typically include the skill set you're looking for and the place someone will occupy in the org chart hierarchy. But remember, the reason you hire someone is to produce some outputs. So why not put that front and center?

Lou Adler has written a great book about revamping your hiring process around this idea, called *Hire With Your Head*. It's geared toward larger companies and the entire hiring process is beyond the scope of this book. But I really like the following quote (emphasis in the original):

...a list of skills and the like is not a job description, it's a person description. A job description is a list of things the person needs to DO to be successful, NOT a list of things the person needs to HAVE.[5]

Start with the list of outputs a successful employee should produce. The entire list is something you'll keep internally, but key parts of it should be part of any job posting you make public. This forces you to be clear about why you're hiring and how that person will be successful. (Adler makes a related point that you should measure success in hiring not on the new hire's first day at work, but a year later when success means both they and their boss are happy that they came on board.)

So rather than saying, "The candidate must have three years of experience in building models in Google Sheets," say, "The person we hire will be building models to predict the best case, worst case, and middle case of each new client that enrolls in our platform. They will be doing models for about six clients a month." This also gives you an objective way to judge the person's performance, which we'll cover next.

OUTPUTS ARE THE ONLY WAY TO JUDGE PERFORMANCE

Improving someone's performance is a major piece of a manager's job. There's no better way to do that than to lay

---

[5] Lou Adler, Hire With Your Head: Using Performance-Based Hiring to Build Great Teams, 4th Edition (Hoboken, NJ: John Wiley & Sons, 2022), 41, Kindle.

out what outputs they're good at producing and which ones they should get better at. By describing their work in terms of outputs, it becomes clear where they can improve and what training they need. If the person wants a promotion, then the outputs they need to produce in their new job should be clear. By seeing their competence in producing those outputs, it becomes obvious when they're ready for the promotion.

There's been a lot written about the pros and cons of performance reviews, different ways to do them, and even whether you should make them formal or not. The biggest benefit to defining job performance with clear outputs is that any review process you use will not be a surprise. If it is, you probably haven't described the outputs in clear, objective terms.

☛ CEO TIME: Review a performance review

Pull up a performance review you've recently given. Look it over and see if it was based on an objective critique of outputs or a subjective impression. Were the qualities you used to judge someone's work adequately communicated in advance?

For example, if the output you wanted was "Prepare a report on XYZ," was it clear to the employee how you'd judge the difference between a good report and a bad one? Or how you'd judge the difference between a good one and a great one?

Does this exercise suggest any changes to how you should do performance reviews in the future?

OUTPUTS MAKE FOR BETTER MENTORING

If someone is surprised by your review of their performance, then something is wrong—and it's not just their performance. When a person knows what outputs they'll be responsible for, they get a pretty good idea of what their performance is like on a regular basis. When you and the employee agree on the outputs they should be producing, your discussion can focus on how to improve and what they need in order to see progress. This can lead to better training or mentoring.

Jonas's title was CFO. But he functioned mostly as a COO, meaning all of the leadership team reported to him. He was frustrated because he had given his key people the title of Director, but that meant different things to him than it did to them. To them, it meant keeping their teams producing their outputs. To him, it meant coming up with innovative ways to increase the output of their teams, and to solve bigger company-wide problems. But he never explained it in terms of the outputs he expected.

This frustration ultimately led to several members of his team feeling like he didn't trust them. Some eventually left the company. Because he never explained what he wanted in terms of output, he was not able to improve their performance. He thought giving them the title of Director should make it obvious what he expected. But it didn't.

If he had explained it properly, he'd have been able to see which of his people were able to naturally perform at what he considered a director level, and who would need mentoring and professional development. Unfortunately, that never happened.

☛ **CEO TIME: See where mentoring is needed**

Who is someone you feel is performing below par? If they were to improve with a wave of your magic wand, what outputs would you see change?

Is there someone in your organization who can mentor them to improve those outputs?

If not, is there a coach or consultant you can hire?

OUTPUTS HELP EVERYONE PLAY AT THE TOP OF THEIR GAME

As director of the Bone and Joint Center at Magee-Womens Hospital in Pittsburgh, PA, Tony DiGioia, M.D. has had an impact far beyond Pittsburgh. He developed a protocol called "patient and family-centered care" (PFCC) which is a method for redesigning the entire patient experience, starting with when people enter the parking lot all the way through to rehabilitation months after surgery. In business we call that designing a workflow from the customer's point of view. It delivers what DiGioia calls the trifecta: better medical outcomes, better patient satisfaction, and reduced costs.

One of his concepts is something he calls "everyone plays at the top of their game." This means that a doctor only does things a doctor is licensed to do. A doctor doesn't do anything a physician's assistant or a nurse practitioner is trained and licensed to do. Those people don't do anything a registered nurse can do. Registered nurses don't do anything a licensed practical nurse can do. And so on.

In the medical world, the different levels of licensing make this division of labor obvious. But you can do the same thing with Output Thinking. You start by specifying the different outputs—usually these are already being produced by someone in your company. Then determine who should be assigned to produce those outputs. In some cases this will be dependent on training. In other cases it will be determined by a level of responsibility in the company. Corporate officers are required to produce (or at least sign off on) certain outputs. Team leaders may be required for others.

This concept of playing at the top of your game can produce many benefits for any business. One is reduced cost. People with less training and lower salaries are reducing the workload of those with more training and higher salaries. If you can design your workflow to do that it can be a huge benefit.

Another benefit is increased job satisfaction. Most people enjoy a challenge and go into their chosen field to do meaningful work. Constantly working below your skill level can be demoralizing, but working at the top of your game is motivating.

A third benefit is providing an obvious career path and setting the stage for targeted training. When people see that by getting more training they can move up, this inspires them to take that training seriously. As they do, it allows you to track who is being trained for what outputs and to develop a training grid.

☛ CEO TIME: Training grid

This is actually an exercise you might want to have your managers do. It's one of the simplest tools I've ever developed. Make a grid. Put a list of outputs down the left column and names across the top. In the cells, put an X when someone is fully trained to produce that output.

It shows you who's trained for what. It also shows in which tasks no one is fully trained. You also can put a P in a cell for the primary person to produce that output and an S for the secondary or backup person. This will show you which outputs have no backup.

	Name 1	Name 2	Name 3
Output 1			
Output 2			
Output 3			

You can also use the training grid to reward or promote people as they get more training. For more ways to use the grid, see this short video: https://decipherpublications.com/output-thinking-extras/.

Use a to-don't list

I'm indebted to Less Antman for this idea. If you're not in a highly regulated profession like medicine, it's likely there's no government agency describing what your junior-level employees are *not* permitted to do. But if you want everyone to play at the top of their game, you'll have to come up with a list of things people at different levels in the company *shouldn't* be doing. One thing that can help is to use a 'to-don't' list. It's another name for a division of labor.

Let me tell you about my mail carrier. His name is Joe. He's a great guy. We've never made an official list, but we do have a strict division of which outputs we each produce. My outputs are to seal the letter, put on adequate postage, and write the address in a legible way. His are to take my output as his input and drive my mail to where it needs to go. The output of my job is the input to his.

What if I didn't do my job? Suppose I didn't have time to write the address and just handed him a blank envelope with verbal instructions. "Joe, it goes to my mother-in-law, Sylvia. She lives in the brick house about a mile down the road from where the Pizza Hut used to be. Same place you delivered her birthday card last year." What do you think would happen? Well, there's no way he'd do the addressing for me. One time he might wait while I addressed the envelope since he's a nice guy and we do tip pretty well at the holidays. But next time he'd just tell me to have it ready for when he came back the next day. Addressing my envelope is on Joe's to-don't list.

When caring can backfire

You want everyone doing what they do best. I'm better at addressing the mail and Joe is better at delivering it. But something I've seen happen in companies where people care a lot is that people will cover for each other and produce someone else's output when that person doesn't do it. They want the output to be done right to make the customers happy.

What's wrong with that? Of course this can be a good thing when someone is temporarily swamped, or makes an occasional mistake. I'm not saying people should be jerks. But if it happens too much it can degrade the whole process of people playing at the top of their game. It can obscure the fact that someone might need more training or better tools or might even be in the wrong job. And it can result in poor performance, or cost overruns by people who are doing something that's not the best use of their skills, even when they care a lot.

That's where a definition of outputs and a to-don't list can help.

☛ CEO TIME: Your to-don't list

Start by keeping a list of everything you do at work for a week. Everything. This activity is annoying to carry out but very beneficial. Then spend your CEO Time reviewing the list. You'll find that the activities fall into three groups. The first two should be on your to-don't list.

1. Outputs that don't need to be produced at all. Great. Stop doing them. BAM! Infinite efficiency, since the most efficient way to do something is not to do it in the first place. But because efficiency is not the same as effectiveness, you'll find many things fall into the next two groups.

2. Outputs that need to be done but are not the best use of your time. Not only do they keep you from playing at the top of your game, they deprive others of the chance to improve. Some of these you're only doing because you can do them quickly or even instinctually and you dread having to train someone else to do them. These are ripe for delegation.

3. Outputs that only you can produce. This is playing at the top of your game.

I will add one nod to the benefit of your position. You might decide to put some things on your to-don't list just because you don't like to do them. Or keep others on your to-do list because you like doing them even if doing them is not playing at the top of your game. Just be aware of the ramifications of when you do this so you don't overuse your privilege.

How do you make sure your employees are playing at the top of their game? By assigning outputs properly.

CHAPTER 6

ASSIGNING OUTPUTS TO PEOPLE

USUALLY OUTPUTS ARE attached to job titles or roles, not people. But it's worse than that: they are *assumed* to be attached to roles. For example, if someone has the title Senior Technician, what outputs do you assume them to be responsible for? Some would say they will be responsible for overseeing a Junior Technician or an apprentice, which makes them a bit of a manager. Others will say they are not on a management track, but they are given more complicated work because they have the training to finish this work on their own.

If you don't assume certain outputs have to be produced by someone with a certain job title, you can be more flexible and take advantage of people's individual strengths and abilities. This can increase the company's overall productivity.

Here's how it works. The first step is to list the outputs that are required for your team or your company's success. Then match them up with your people's strengths and abilities. Try to assign outputs to the lowest level person who can produce them. This helps everyone play at the top of their game.

Here's an example. Michael used to be my collections person. He would have to reach out to delinquent accounts and get them to pay their past due bills. So the required output was money collected, as measured by a decrease in past due accounts. It wasn't his full-time job; he had other outputs he was responsible for as well. But he was fantastic at collections—as long as he did it on the phone. People loved him, which is not something you hear very often about the person calling for money.

However, Michael was terrible with email. His writing was sloppy, and his spelling was atrocious. At first we said he was not allowed to hit send before someone else had reviewed the email (and usually rewritten it). But that grew too cumbersome. So we took away from him the output of doing collections by email. Luckily most of the customers were reachable by phone. But on the occasion where an email was needed, that was assigned to someone else. That's a very unusual division of labor for a collections person. And in a different company it would be unmanageable. But it worked for us.

Here's another example. Suppose you have multiple salespeople. You need some way to divide up territories so each one has their own set of prospects they're working with. Some companies do this by geography, or alphabetically by company name, or on a rotating basis based on when the prospect entered the sales pipeline. But you could also see what kind of sales each person is best at, and assign the work that way. One may be better at up-selling to existing customers, while another is great at landing a first sale from a new customer. This is a more granular breakdown of the output than just "sales." By knowing your people and matching them with the outputs they do well, you can make them more successful.

ONE PERSON AND MANY OUTPUTS IS NORMAL

Remember Larry functioning as a team leader and producing the output of a more effective team? As you can imagine, it's not a full-time job to be the team leader of a small framing crew. He didn't just stand around leaning on his shovel and smoking cigarettes the rest of the time. Larry also cut lumber and pounded some nails himself. Larry was producing two outputs without realizing it: the frames themselves, and the team to work on the frames.

It's very common for team leaders to work as part of the crew as well. In other words, that same person produces two outputs. One as crew leader, and because leading the crew is not usually a full-time job, they also perform as part-time crew members.

For Larry, it didn't stop there. As the business owner, he was also the sales guy. That output was producing enough business to keep the company afloat. And he sent the invoices and paid the bills. It's very common for company owners to feel overwhelmed by the number of different outputs they are responsible for—until they get good at systemizing and delegating. We'll cover how to do that in the section on systems.

In companies of every size, most people produce multiple outputs, even if they are not the owner. Sometimes these outputs are related to the job title you'll see on the org chart, and sometimes they are not (remember Bill the receptionist who also did IT support?).

USE OUTPUTS *BEFORE* YOU PROMOTE

Bill the receptionist was not transitioning into doing IT support full-time. But sometimes you want someone to grow into a new role.

One advantage of assigning outputs to people, not roles, is that it makes it very easy to promote people. You can basically assign them important outputs that are needed in their new position. You can do this on a temporary or project basis to see how they do before you make the promotion. Obviously you have to give them training and time to do the work, so you can't just dump it on their existing jobs without making changes. But if it doesn't work out, it's much easier to dial back than if you'd given them a new title and the raise that goes with it.

When you do this, don't lock the assignments into the new job title. It reminds me of a story about a multinational company. For some reason, all the French translation was done on a different floor away from the people who did translation into other languages. It was rather inconvenient, but no one knew why. Finally someone got to the bottom of it. When the company started to expand overseas, the first country they did business in was France. Only one person knew French and she worked on that floor, so all the French translation was routed to her. And it grew from there. The problem was that as the company grew, that output was never reassigned.

This process can be as formal or informal as is appropriate for your situation. Earlier I mentioned Lori and her husband Troy, who had retail stores in LA and Atlanta. They are not typical business types—she's an actress and he's an artist. But they've done well. Partly because they've surrounded themselves with people who are good at the things they are not great at. After they opened their sixth store, they realized they needed another layer of coordination between themselves and the store managers.

But they were struggling with exactly what that person would do. In typical org chart thinking, they started talking about this person as the Operations Manager. It's typical in a retail chain like this that the person over the store managers is called a District Manager, but the title doesn't matter. I encouraged them to ignore the title and focus on the outputs they were producing that they wanted to offload. One of their store managers, Emma, was showing real promise. But she didn't want the job. However, Emma was really good at using a certain type of software they used for staying in touch with customers after the sale. So Lori asked her to visit each store and train their people on this software. (Training is an output.) Then they gave Emma the authority to oversee the usage of that software at every store. (Oversight is also an output.)

After making the rounds doing this, Emma got excited about the possibility of becoming the Operations

Manager overseeing all the stores. So they had her come up with a transition plan that listed the different outputs Emma would be taking on over nine months. It showed when they'd need to hire a replacement store manager and how much time Emma would spend training her replacement. Seeing almost two dozen outputs and the timing of the shift, Lori and Emma both knew that this was a smart way to go. Emma's plan was accepted without any major changes and she started taking over some of those outputs, but didn't get the official promotion for six months.

Here's the best part. Many of these outputs were ones that Lori was producing, so it freed up her time to do more strategic work. But many were things that hadn't been done particularly well. Emma brought outputs to her new job that had been lacking before.

☛ CEO TIME: Promotion

Think of someone you'd like to groom for promotion. List the outputs they would have to produce to succeed in their new position.

Then rate their proficiency in producing each one.

If there are some outputs you're not sure they have the capacity to produce, think about a project you can use to test their ability or as a training exercise to expand their skills.

Don't forget to list the outputs they are currently producing and consider who can take those over as the person you're promoting grows into their new role.

The way Lori worked with Emma is a more structured (and I'll suggest more effective) way to promote someone than usually happens in an SMB. More typical is that you notice someone "has potential." You think they're "a real go-getter." They don't wait to be told what to do; they just figure it out. So you start to consider them for a promotion.

Beware! You're about to fall into the trap of shadow outputs.

SHADOW OUTPUTS HINDER COMPANY GROWTH

Shadow outputs are outputs that someone produces which aren't officially a part of their job (like Bill, the receptionist). You'll often hear a person who produces these shadow outputs described as a hustler. It feels good working with them—they make your job easier. You'd think that would be a good thing. And it is good for the moment, but it's not good for the future.

When you look at a situation like this through the lens of Output Thinking, this person may be providing a critical output that no one recognizes until they're not doing it anymore. It can mask a deficiency in your organization. Or it can divert some people's work away from playing at the top of their game toward what's most urgent. Often what's really happening is they're producing a whole bunch of outputs that are in a realm I call shadow outputs.

Perhaps your office manager is really good at proofreading and catches a lot of typos in marketing materials before they go out the door. Perhaps one of your programmers cleans up the design specs for every project she works on. Maybe your bookkeeper happens to know Portuguese and can translate the customer support problems that come in from Brazil.

Outputs that aren't officially recognized are shadow outputs

It's not that shadow outputs shouldn't be done. And it's not even that they need to be related to the person's job title. The problem occurs when they're unknown. The work gets done and things move smoothly. But then you want to promote someone, and they no longer have the time to produce the shadow outputs you didn't know about. From there, things don't go as smoothly because their replacement doesn't do those things that were under the radar. Or their official job becomes more demanding and the shadow outputs get shortchanged.

Output Thinking helps you uncover all the outputs that are required so you can grow your company properly.

Here's a story of what happened when someone's shadow outputs got in the way of her career path. Tanya Reilly is a senior principal engineer at Squarespace who's written about career development for people with technical skills. On her No Idea blog, tells the story of a software engineer (let's call her Julia) who sees some gaps in the organization that are delaying the project she's working on. So she jumps in and fixes them, then gets passed over for a promotion because she has not spent enough time actually writing code. Reilly calls what Julia was doing "glue work," helping the team work more effectively. Her point is that no one asked her to do it. And even though she helped the project move forward, she delayed the advancement of her own career. Here's the key paragraph from Reilly that details the output that's expected from this glue:

> Your job title says "software engineer," but you seem to spend most of your time in meetings. You'd like to have time to code, but nobody else is onboarding the junior engineers, updating the roadmap, talking to the users, noticing the things that got dropped, asking questions on design documents, and making sure that everyone's going roughly in the same direction. If you stop doing those things, the team won't be as successful ... If this describes you, congratulations: you're the glue.[6]

Looking at this problem through the lens of Output Thinking, here's my take. This is a classic case of shadow outputs. What Reilly calls glue, I call management. It was lacking and Julia saw the gap and (unlike Larry's crew) jumped in to help. Here are the outputs she produced:

- junior engineers onboarded
- roadmap updated
- dropped items picked up
- design questions asked
- everyone aligned
- a more successful team

---

[6] https://noidea.dog/glue

These outputs, though necessary for the ultimate success of the project, weren't in Julia's job title: they were shadow outputs. And because of that, she lost out on her promotion. That to me is bad management, in two ways. First, someone should have known this project needed those outputs and assigned them to someone. Second, Julia's manager should have recognized her outputs, discussed with her if she wanted to continue to provide them or not, and then reassessed her job to suit the project's needs and her career goals.

☛ CEO TIME: Expose the shadow outputs

Think of someone in your company that you consider to be a real go-getter. List all the outputs they produce that you know about. Talk to them (and their boss if that's not you) to see if there are more outputs you were unaware of. Add them to the list. Then consider these questions:

- How many of those outputs are not officially part of their job (i.e. shadow outputs)?
- Are any of the outputs preventing them from playing at the top of their game?
- Are any preventing other people from playing at the top of their games?
- Should you reassign any outputs or change any roles?
- When this person gets promoted (or leaves), how will you be sure that all the outputs they were producing get covered?

If you understand all the outputs a person is producing and all the skills it takes to produce those outputs, you can do a better job of tailoring their responsibilities to their unique mix of strengths and weaknesses, and ensure that there are no gaps in your organization.

CHAPTER 7

MANAGER OUTPUTS

THE PREVIOUS STORY is important because it highlights a very common phenomenon: missing management. Whoever designed the team that Julia was on thought that people would produce all the required outputs without management. We saw the same thing with Larry when he added new crews to his framing company, but didn't put a team leader in place. To properly address this issue we first need to define management.

Management is getting work done through other people

The simplicity of this definition makes it look easy. But it isn't. There are two parts to this definition: the work and the people. Both of these are enhanced by Output Thinking. As a manager, your job is to help people do better work and to align that work with the strategy and direction of the company. The work is not the effort they put in, but the outputs they produce. Alignment means they are producing outputs that matter.

As for the people part, a manager's job is to help people do good work. They do this by providing tools, training, incentives, connections to others in the company, motivation, and anything else a person needs to produce good outputs. But unless and until those outputs are specified, all the tools and training and the like won't be sufficient.

In other words, a good manager monitors the work and supports the people. Old-school managers thought they managed by making sure people put in the time at work. But good managers manage the output, not the activity. That's true whether someone is working across from your desk, across the hall, or across the ocean. The output of management is the same whether the people they manage are in the building or remote.

Good management starts by defining what outputs someone needs to produce. Typically the people who work most closely with customers or do physical work have the easiest outputs to define. Someone making widgets, or who fulfills work orders, or who closes deals produces very measurable outputs.

It gets a bit more complicated as you move up the company hierarchy into management. But this is often where it's most important to define outputs, otherwise you may fall prey to the "Peter Principle." This phrase was coined by Laurence Peter, a Canadian educator who studied hierarchy in organizations. His principle states: "In a hierarchy, every employee tends to rise to his level of incompetence." What he meant is that people who do a good job get promoted. But often the new job requires different outputs and if the person doesn't have the skills to produce those outputs, it's rare that they get demoted. Instead, they remain in a job they can't do as well as the job they got promoted from. This leads to Peter's corollary: "In time, every post tends to be occupied by an employee who is incompetent to carry out its duties."[7]

The book, The Peter Principle, was written as a satire but rang so true for how things work in large organizations that it became a bestseller and was translated into 38 languages! The most common example of Peter's principle in SMBs happens when a great salesperson gets promoted to sales manager. But the skills needed in those roles are different because the outputs required from each job are different. The output of a salesperson is sales, revenue, and signed deals. The output of a sales manager is a well-functioning team that produces sales, revenue, and signed deals. It takes very different skills to help a team produce what you had been producing as a salesperson. You sometimes also see this in sports, where a star player does not make a good coach or manager.

DEFINING OUTPUTS IS IMPORTANT FOR TEAMWORK

When we talked before about micromanagement, we discussed that people need definite outputs defined in

---

[7] Laurence J. Peter and Raymond Hull, The Peter Principle: Why Things Always Go Wrong (United Kingdom: Profile Books Limited, 2020).

non-arbitrary ways. But there's more to it. We have this idea that if we hire good people and leave them alone, they'll figure it all out. Maybe this came from management consultant Jim Collins, who said the most important thing is to get the right people on the bus. Maybe it came from Peter Drucker. He's the guy who coined the term knowledge worker and said, "The knowledge worker cannot be supervised closely or in detail, he must direct himself."[8] (In Drucker's world, workers were almost always men. He originally published this in 1967.)

We know the idea of self-direction doesn't work with teams in the physical world. Imagine getting some carpenters, plumbers, and electricians all together and saying, "I want you to figure out how to build this house. We don't have any blueprints, but I have a picture of what it's supposed to look like from this magazine. Also, I'm not going to be doing any scheduling because you're smart folks and I'm sure you'll work it out."

That doesn't make sense for knowledge workers any more than it does for people in the building trades. In order for very smart people to work as a unit they need the support of management to define what their output should look like and how it should integrate with other people in the organization, and to provide them with tools like schedules, specifications, workflows, and other inputs that they need to do good work.

Without those tools, if people need some help, they end up interrupting each other with incessant emails and

---

[8] Peter F. Drucker, The Effective Executive: The Definitive Guide to Getting the Right Things Done (New York, NY: HarperCollins, 2004), 4.

meetings that waste time because they lack a clear definition of what the output of a good job looks like. It's your job as a manager to provide these good, smart people you hired with the support they need to be effective. I'm not talking about training—though that's important too. I'm talking about these things:

1. A clear description of what the output of good work looks like. Knowledge work often means making decisions, so be sure to include decisions in this description of the output.

2. A schedule or prioritization so your people know what to work on when in order for them to be productive to the rest of the organization.

3. Workflows (which are diagramed when appropriate).

4. Communication protocols, so people have time to get deep work done without interruptions but can still get the help they need from others.

Productivity cannot be left to the individual, especially when people work together. Teams need workflows to be designed and structures within which people can be most effective. It is the manager's job to provide these if they want to maximize productivity. When you do this, you'll often track the output from the entire team, not each individual.

If you manage people, I say this is your job because it's your responsibility as a manager. I don't mean to say you are the one to figure it out sitting alone in an ivory tower and delivering the message from on high. Often others on your team will have better ideas than you do about some of these things. But they don't have the perspective you do of how their work fits into the bigger picture of the entire organization. I encourage you to collaborate to craft a description of the outputs you expect from each person, so that you can achieve the goal of getting good work done through other people.

In some cases, there may be no one on your team who's good at developing a workflow diagram or a value map, for example. That's when you bring in an outside consultant. Then make sure you institutionalize the results; everybody that needs to have access to the information also must be able to find it easily and quickly. And keep things flexible. Expect that there will be improvements and changes.

THREE LEVELS OF MANAGEMENT

You may think you should judge the output of a manager by the output of their team, and you would not be wrong. But there's more to it than that. We also need to look at the output of the managers themselves, and we can categorize management outputs into three distinct types that I call the three levels of management.

Level 1: Team leader

In some industries the term "team leader" is used, in others "supervisor" or "crew chief." Regardless of the title, this person is in charge of a small crew or team and is usually also a worker. They are responsible for decisions such as scheduling, making sure the crew has enough supplies, quality control, etc. But they usually can't change the direction or makeup of the crew, make major decisions about the crew's assignments, or hire or fire people. The team leader is typically given a task for the crew to perform, then organizes the crew to accomplish the task. But usually the team leader can't modify the task in any significant way.

The output of a good team leader is a more effective team. They make sure the team members have what they need to do a good job. That starts with a clear understanding of what a good job looks like: the outputs that constitute good work. But people need more than clarity. They need tools, training, and time to do good work. Sometimes they need connections to others in the organization, and sometimes they need protection from wasteful meetings or other activities that keep them from doing good work. Providing people with what they need to do a great job: this is the main output of a good team leader.

Level 2: Executive or middle management
Managers at this level are responsible for allocating resources to accomplish something. They are usually given goals or projects and they prioritize the tasks needed to accomplish those goals. Then they determine ways that the project can be accomplished within constraints of budget, staffing levels, equipment, etc. The outputs of people at this level are priorities, assignments, budgets, problem-solving, and similar types of decisions.

In smaller SMBs, level 2 management is often done off the cuff based on situational needs. If the organization is small enough, that's sufficient. But as the company scales, you need more rigor at this level. In larger organizations, middle management is also responsible for coordination between different groups, departments, or teams. In these cases, one output of the manager is the influence they have to work with their peers.

Someone once said about construction that the supervisor's job is to keep the crew on task, while the project manager's job is to keep the project on budget. I think that shows the difference between level 1 and level 2 managers pretty well. However, when it comes to deciding what projects the company should take on, that's where level 3 management is needed.

Level 3: Upper management

This level of management is responsible for setting the strategic direction of the company. What exactly is strategy? It's best defined by Roger Martin, the former Dean of the Rotman School of Management at the University of Toronto. He said strategy is deciding where you will play and how you will win. What he means is deciding which markets to be in (where you'll play) and how to provide value to those customers (how you'll win). Those decisions are the essence of strategy, and remember, decisions are outputs.

Upper management is also concerned with things like how to best raise capital and utilize funds. They make decisions about which products to carry and which to drop, and how to address trends in the marketplace.

Profitability goals and long-term versus short-term trade-offs are the purview of this level of management, as are exit strategy decisions. These decisions are best made with lots of input from others in the company. But ultimately, managers at this level make the call. In an SMB that's usually the CEO/owner.

The outputs of upper-level management include a clear strategic direction for the company along with plans and resources to achieve that strategy.

First-level managers tend to ask When? What? and Where? because they are responsible for getting stuff done. Middle managers ask How? and Who? because they are given a goal and have to muster resources and assign them, often within budgetary constraints. Top-level managers ask WHY? because they are responsible for the strategic purpose of what is being done.

Smaller organizations spend most of their management efforts at level 1, almost none at level 2 and at times some at level 3. This allocation of management resources changes as companies grow and strategy and planning become more important.

As those management resources change, it can affect the cost structure of the organization and require changes to the business model. I was talking with the VP of a web development company with about 100 employees. He had been there when the company started and told me they used to be able to create a website for around $5,000. Now, he said, with so many employees they couldn't touch one for under $20,000. But we agreed that his customer base and offerings had improved as well. Companies that hired them now wanted 24/7 support and security features. Those customers would be scared to death to have a website done by somebody working alone for only $5k. So it's quite possible to adapt to a different cost structure as long as you upgrade your pricing and the market you serve at the same time.

Larger companies might have more than three layers of managers, but if you look at the outputs they produce, you'll see those outputs occupy one of these three levels. Much like a large restaurant might have a pastry chef and a chocolate chef who both produce desserts. Levels? Layers? Vocabulary fails, but if you consider the outputs you need it becomes clear who does what.

☛ CEO TIME: Track your management time

As the owner of an SMB, you may be involved at all three levels of management. A useful exercise is to track your management time according to the type of management output you produce.

Are you keeping a team on track and more productive? Level 1.

Are you allocating resources or assigning people? Level 2.

Are you making strategic decisions? Level 3.

As the owner, you are the only person who can be the ultimate decision-maker at level 3. If you are doing level 1 and 2 management, you should be thinking of what others could take off your plate.

Dan's company had about 65 people running computer-driven machines to make parts out of metal (5-axis CNC machines, to be exact). They were grouped into teams based on the types of parts they were producing. And Dan had taken the first step in assigning one person on each team to be the team leader. But when he told me some of those teams were doing well and some were not, I met with the team leaders as a group. It turned out that beyond the title, they'd been given no training about what was expected of them or how they should do it. This is not uncommon. In my experience, most people moving into management for the first time in SMB companies don't get the level of training they need.

The solution is to make sure their training covers these things:

- What are the outputs of the team they are responsible for?

- How are those outputs expected to change with them as team leader?

- What will change about their personal outputs? (Team leaders usually produce some of the same outputs they did as a team member—just fewer of them— as they also need time to do the work of leading the team, like producing schedules, providing supplies, etc.)

- Most importantly, the communication skills needed as a team leader.

CEO OUTPUTS

The ultimate manager of a company is the CEO. So what does a CEO do? The question is misleading because it doesn't properly distinguish between the title (CEO) and the outputs they produce. A better question is what outputs does a CEO produce? The outputs I mentioned above in level 3 management are typically produced by the person with the title of CEO.

One other output of the CEO is to coordinate the work of everyone else. (In larger companies, that output is produced by someone with the title COO or President.) I liken it to a conductor of a symphony orchestra. Did you ever notice that the conductor of an orchestra doesn't make any of the music that the audience came to hear? Yet when she walks out on stage before a single note has been played, she gets an applause. The CEO function is like that. An orchestra conductor creates an environment where each musician contributes their best. And the conductor blends it all together so everyone is playing in tune, in time, and at the right volume to express what the composer wanted when they wrote the piece. The composer's score is analogous to the strategy of the company set by top management.

In an SMB, the person with the title CEO is often the owner. But if you look at the outputs a typical owner produces, you'll see they are not all CEO-level outputs. That's because unless the company is large or going through a really turbulent time, producing CEO outputs is not a full-time job. In smaller SMBs, the person called

CEO often spends a lot of their time in production, sales, or finance.

Here are some times when, even in a small company, the CEO role requires full-time effort:

- during the start-up stage
- when negotiating the sale of the company
- when you have to adapt to a changing market
- executing an acquisition
- adapting the organizational structure because of growth

If your company doesn't need a full-time CEO then you have more options if you've got other people to produce all the outputs the company needs on a daily basis. You can spend your time producing other outputs. Or you can take time away from the company if you want. The way to do this is to make sure your non-CEO outputs are handled well by other people. This is how you start to remove yourself from the day-to-day routine, since level 3 management functions are rarely urgent.

CHAPTER 8

OUTPUTS COME FROM SYSTEMS

UNTIL YOU CAN hire a workforce of elves, your outputs are produced by people. (Even AI still needs people to write the prompts.) If you don't want your company to grow, it may be sufficient to find people who can produce all the required outputs by brute force or natural talent. However, to grow, those outputs need to be systemized.

A grandmother who makes great food without following a recipe is producing the right output. She's spent years learning how to do it well so she doesn't need a recipe. But she's not using a repeatable system. As long as she's healthy, and in the kitchen, the food is terrific. But the process is locked in her head. If she was your chef in a restaurant, you could never open a second one that would produce the same quality of food.

Systemization is the way to produce outputs that are repeatable and scalable.

SYSTEMIZATION MAKES OUTPUTS REPEATABLE AND SCALABLE

Systemization is often considered the holy grail in organizing a company, particularly a privately held one. Michael Gerber coined the phrase "work on your business, not in it" to distinguish between people owning a business and just owning a job. He used McDonald's as an example. Not because their burgers are so great, but because they have a system for making burgers that is repeatable and scalable. Gerber says that business owners should constantly be asking themselves, "How can I get my business to work, but without me?" That is the essence of systemization.

Gerber set out that concept in his 1995 book *The E-Myth Revisited: Why Most Small Businesses Don't Work and What to Do About It*, which was groundbreaking at the time. But he left it to the reader to figure out how to do it. Since systemizing my own companies and working with so many others, I've learned several important benefits that systemization can deliver:

- It's repeatable: identical outputs can be produced again and again.
- It's scalable: more people can produce more results.
- It's fixable: you can see if a process is going off the rails and make corrections before the final result is finished.

- It's trainable: you can use the system to train others.

- It's cost-effective: let's face it, grandmothers are expensive. With a good system you can have lower-cost people do some (or sometimes all) of the work.

McDonald's doesn't hire great hamburger chefs. Instead they've devised a system where anyone of any age or background can be trained to make a McBurger. My friend Jon Matzner, who writes a newsletter about extreme outsourcing, calls this the stoned teenager effect. McDonald's is so systemized that even a stoned teenager can produce the right output.

Don't get me wrong. I actually like McDonald's. It was the first place I drove to when I got my driver's license. Here's a quote that applies to McDonald's even though it's really about the lean manufacturing system that was devised by Toyota to make cars:

> Brilliant process management is our strategy. We get brilliant results from average people managing brilliant processes. We observe that our competitors often get average (or worse) results from brilliant people managing broken processes.
>
> **—DANIEL T. JONES, CHAIRMAN OF THE LEAN ENTERPRISE ACADEMY**

If you want to produce outputs in a repeatable way, you need good processes or systems. And they need to be well documented. To be able to do that, we need to look at the parts that make up a system.

THE PARTS OF A SYSTEM

Every system has four parts. We've been talking about one of them—the output. Producing the output is the reason the system exists, while the three other parts make it repeatable and scalable. Work that produces an output is often called a system, an SOP (standard operating procedure), a process, or even a task. For our purposes, those words are pretty much interchangeable.

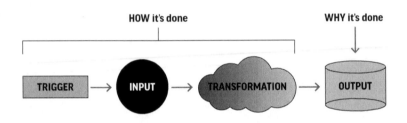

Let's use a payroll system to illustrate.

- **Trigger** = the day you do payroll.
- **Input** = hours and wages of employees for the pay period.
- **Transformation** = the calculations usually performed by a payroll service.
- **Output** = money to people's bank accounts, reports and tax forms.

Here it is in more detail.

The TRIGGER is what starts the process. For payroll, it's a day (like every other Thursday). On that date the data for the prior pay period is sent to the payroll company. Other processes have a different trigger. A fulfillment system is triggered when a customer makes a purchase. The air-conditioning system is triggered when the temperature reaches a certain point. A reordering process is triggered when inventory reaches a certain level.

When systemizing your company, it's important to note the trigger so everyone involved knows if and when the system should be activated.

The INPUT is what people need in order to operate the system. For payroll, it's the list of people's pay rates, the hours they worked, the time they took off during that pay period, etc. If your system makes cakes, the input is the ingredients and equipment required. You can think of the input as the necessary requirements before the system can be effective. There's no point in starting to bake a cake if you can't use the oven today or if you don't have enough flour.

We'll see later that the input of one system could be output from a previous system.

The TRANSFORMATION is what happens to change the input into the output. It's what we normally think of as the work people do. People take the system's input and transform it into the output. This is the part that's commonly documented in standard operating procedures and training. This is where processes and procedures live.

When people talk about systemizing their companies, they most often are referring to this transformation step. Documenting the transformation is getting the knowledge of how to make a cake out of your grandmother's head and onto a recipe card. Recording the instructions for the transformation is obviously important, but if the other three parts aren't documented as well, your documentation will be insufficient.

The OUTPUT is the result. It's the point at which the system has completed its run. For payroll, it's money going to employees, reports to management, and tax forms and money going to the government. This is a description of what you expect to see when the output is produced. It should include the necessary attributes (like quantity and quality) of outputs that we discussed in chapter 4.

CHAPTER 9

HOW TO DOCUMENT YOUR SYSTEMS

WITH WELL-DOCUMENTED SYSTEMS your company can produce output repeatedly with no loss of quality. Here's how to do it.

DOCUMENT THE SYSTEM AND THE INSTANCE DIFFERENTLY

Before we get into how to actually write the documentation, I want to clear up something that often gets confused. There's a difference between documenting how an output is produced and tracking an instance of it being produced.

When a system is not very mature (meaning work is accomplished by individuals using intuition and knowledge in their heads without a written process), then it's easy to comingle the two. But if you're scaling your company, you want to keep them separate. To show you an example of what I mean, let's head back to the kitchen.

Now we're running a German restaurant and making sauerbraten. It's a dish that requires meat to be marinated for up to two weeks and then cooked for several hours. To have it on our menu, we need to have multiple batches going at once so there's always some ready to serve.

The recipe is the documentation of the process. It includes the four parts: trigger, input, transformation, output. The transformation is the part that takes two weeks. Our recipe might include variations for weekends as that's when you may sell more sauerbraten. That means two weeks ahead you have to make a different amount, so the trigger of the recipe includes checking the date. Other than that it's a pretty straightforward recipe.

The instances, however, are a different story. Each batch is a separate instance. It's weighed and measured, put in a bin and labeled. You might have fourteen different batches in the walk-in refrigerator at any one time— each started on a different date and ready at a different time. You'd need to know how old each one is, which one is ready for the oven, etc. That information is tracked in a different place from the recipe. It could be as simple as putting a strip of tape on each bin with the date it was started. For more complex systems, you might track more data (like the source of ingredients) with barcodes and a database or a full-fledged ERP (enterprise resource planning) software to keep track of all the instances.

Here's another example: your sales system. As a prospect moves through different stages of your sales pipeline, your team does different things based on the stage they are at, such as:

- Send more information.
- Ask about their budget and approval process.
- Schedule a demo.
- Prepare a quote.
- Offer credit (if approved).

How to perform each piece and when it should be done will be documented in your sales training documents. But the instances of each sale are captured in your CRM (customer relationship management) software. This one is a little more variable than sauerbraten because each prospect moves forward in the sales pipeline at a different speed, and some even move backward. Their progress will be reflected in your CRM, not in your sales training.

It's a bit of an oversimplification to say it this way, but the documentation is for training how to do the process and the instances are for managing the process in action. You track instances differently from the documentation. However, there is a connection between the two.

No process is frozen in time. It changes as people learn better ways to do things. Where do they learn those improvements? Usually from the instances of performing the process out in the wild. So you need a way to keep the process in sync with the real world or it will be worse than useless. It's actually harmful to have out-of-date documentation because it erodes trust in the system and encourages inconsistency of operations.

The simplest way to do this is to have a process to check the processes. For each process, schedule a review on a regular basis. How often you perform the review varies with the frequency of the process. When it's time to do the review, have the people who actually do the work review what's written and make any updates. You really should encourage people to update the documents any time there's an improvement in how things are done. But a regularly scheduled update is a good backstop.

HOW DOCUMENTATION SHOULD LOOK

Here's what your documentation should look like. It will normally be a written document with links to video or other media. They are both important. Video and other visuals are often easier to follow, but written documents are easier to change and search. You need both.

Each system or process needs a name. It's what you call the system or task that produces the output. Name them in simple phrases that generally include verbs. Josh Schultz is president/COO of CaneKast, a company that buys and runs non-ferrous foundries in the US. In that position he's in charge of systemizing the company. Here's his advice on naming systems:

> When I name these, I name them [using] the sentence I would say to someone if I wanted it done. This makes them easy to search later for anyone at the company. If you ask yourself, "What would someone search for if they needed to do this procedure?" That is what you

should name it. Not something like Billing -> Invoice 2.3 [rather] Invoice the Customers.[9]

These names are not job titles or roles. They are more specific than that. To use Josh's example, someone may have the job title of bookkeeper but they'd perform a task called *Invoice the Customer* and the output they produce would be invoices. Unless you need so many invoices that a person would spend 40 hours a week producing them, that bookkeeper would perform other tasks too.

Here's an example of what documenting an invoicing system (or SOP) might look like, with my comments in brackets.

INVOICING CUSTOMERS

Updated 2020-03-10 By Jane Smith (in preparation for everyone going remote)

Written 2019-05-24 By Jane Smith

Purpose: This system gets invoices out to customers in a timely fashion so we can collect funds as soon as possible.

Trigger—Biweekly with Exceptions
We cut invoices every other Thursday. However, when a job is completed in excess of $10,000, we cut the invoice the same day the job was finished.

---

[9] Josh Schultz, "SMB Ops Letter: How to Write a Procedure That Works!," joshuaschultz.com, January 5, 2023, https://www. joshuaschultz.com/blog/how-to-write-a-procedure.

Input—Job Forms

Completed job forms are used as the inputs to the invoices. They must be signed by the team leader who did the work and by the customer approving the work.

Transformation—How to Invoice Customers

1. First sort all the job orders by customer. Then we can send a single invoice to the customer that includes multiple jobs as line items in the invoice.

2. Open QuickBooks.

3. If there are any new customers add them to the customer center. [Link to video goes here - this video shows how to add a new customer in QuickBooks. It's screen capture with voice over]

4. Once all the new customers are in, follow these steps to create and send invoices. [Invoices are sent by email to the customer from QuickBooks.]

5. [Link to video - this video shows how to cut an invoice in QuickBooks]

6. When all the invoices have been created and sent, mark the completed job forms and file them in the customer's folders.

Output

This System is finished when all the invoices have been sent by email and completed job forms are filed. The total dollar amount invoiced will show up on the aging report under CURRENT.

Let's look at each part of the document in detail.

Header (or metadata)

It's useful if this is in a box or a highlighted area. It should include the following:

> **Name:** this is the name of the system or the process. Where possible it's also the name of any files associated with it (video files, for example). Use conversational language that can be easily found by searching. And use a unique name for each system.
>
> **Last updated:** when this documentation was last updated.
>
> **By whom:** the person who updated it and/or is responsible for this system.
>
> (Often all the names and dates of all the previous updates are kept in case they're needed for reference.)
>
> **Purpose:** a few sentences explaining why and how this system should be used. It's analogous to the "commander's intent" in a military order. It allows the person operating the system to have some leeway to adapt to unusual circumstances and still accomplish the desired output.

Trigger

This is the start of the system: what sets it off. Sometimes it's a date (payroll every other Thursday) or a condition (inventory level down to X) or an event (customer has placed an order).

Input

This is what the system acts upon: the things you need in order to get started. In a recipe it's the list of ingredients and kitchen equipment you need. Often this is the output of a previous system in the workflow (like the beautifully addressed letter I give to my mail carrier). It's impossible or useless to start the system if all the inputs aren't ready.

Transformation

This part includes instructions of how the work is done to convert the input into the output. There are three basic types of transformations:

- **A recipe.** This is a very detailed step-by-step explanation of what to do. Both the output and the steps of how to produce it are listed in depth.

- **A dance.** This is a process involving another person and reacting to that person's reactions to what you do. You generally can't predefine the steps used to achieve the output, but you can define the output in detail.

- **A creation.** When a creation is required, you can't describe the exact output or the steps used to create it, but you can describe the constraints within which the creation must take place.

There are some processes that combine these different types of transformation. For example, an accountant might devise a tax strategy—this is a creation process (constrained by tax laws). Then they'd fill out the right forms. Filling out the tax forms is a recipe-type SOP.

Usually it's more efficient to separate these processes into two different SOPs performed by different people, each playing at the top of their game.

Every system should have as much detail as possible, with links to videos and other media as appropriate. It should be simple enough that it can be used for training a new person on the job. You may need some if/then choices, such as, "If the invoice is more than $10,000 then do this, otherwise do that."

The purpose of a well-documented system is to get the wisdom and insight out of people's heads and written down so it's repeatable and scalable. Melissa Withers runs an investment firm, RevUp, that invests in companies at the scale-up stage. She summed it up beautifully when she called it moving your company from people to process.

Let's look at the three types of transformations in more detail.

Documenting a Recipe SOP

A recipe should have step-by-step instructions. It should include checklists and video or other media as appropriate. A recipe is similar to a computer algorithm.

The body of the document should have lots of headings that are easy to scan.

- Use bullet points
- Use a numbered sequence
- Use checklists

You probably need more detail than you think. When an intuitive person is producing an output, they often do things based on experience and judgment that seem like they can't be explained. But surprisingly often, they can be.

Cookbooks, for example, are very detailed. They tell you exactly how much of each ingredient to use, whether to slice or dice your onions, and give exact times and temperatures. Many jobs need an SOP with this level of detail.

Here's an example I adapted from a presentation I recently attended by Justin Vogt. Suppose you have a list of 10,000 companies from the same industry you want to send a letter to in order to start a business relationship. But you want to customize each letter so you don't sound like a total jerk. And you know that most of those 10,000 aren't right for you anyway—maybe only 500 or 1,000 are. You could look at the websites of each company and very quickly decide which ones you should eliminate. But doing that for 10,000 companies wouldn't be the best use of your time.

You can imagine two things.

1. There is a lot of judgment involved. This would be expensive to replicate.

2. The more steps in this process that can be handled by someone without the experience and judgment you have, the faster (and cheaper) it will be.

You need a way to translate your judgment into an algorithm or recipe so someone else can narrow down the list to a manageable size. So you check out a few of the websites of companies on the list. You pay attention to what makes you eliminate or include certain companies from the list. Here's what you realize:

- Certain geographies are off the list, and certain ones make the cut.

- Certain phrases on the website (like *distributor* or *subsidiary of*) indicate companies you don't want to bother with.

- If the name of the owner or CEO is listed, that's a bonus—you'll use that to look them up on LinkedIn for possible connections you can mention in the letter.

Now you've got a way to translate your judgment into an algorithm. Here are the steps you use to tell someone else how to narrow down the list.

1. Start with the first company on the list.

2. Look up the company's website.

3. Eliminate it if you see these words ...

4. Eliminate it if the company is outside of this geography ...

5. If the CEO or owner's name is listed, include it and put the company name and address in list A.

6. If the CEO or owner's name is not listed, include the company name and address in list B.

7. Repeat steps 1–7 till the list is done.

8. Send me both lists in a spreadsheet with the following columns ...

That's the level of detail that's required in a recipe SOP. Just like a cookbook. You could even divide up the list and give those instructions to multiple people if you needed to get through it quickly.

Here's a tip. If your work is intuitive it may seem instantaneous; then separate it into steps. Some of those steps can be made into an algorithm and handed off (either to another person or to a piece of software). If you can't explain it in that level of detail, talk it through with someone else. Often they can see things in your thought process that you can't.

You may think this contradicts what I said before about Output Thinking being the antidote to micromanagement. The way to tell the difference is to ask if it needs to be done to produce the proper output. If it does and you can reduce the process to a recipe (like McDonald's does) then it's not micromanagement; it's a way of pushing the work down in the organization.

A recipe SOP is great when you're dealing with machines, computers, and data. But when you're dealing with people, you need to dance.

Documenting a Dance SOP

Peter Lohmann runs a property management company in Columbus, Ohio. He thinks like an engineer so his processes are well documented. But he told me he uses different departments to deal with operations (machines, computers, and maintenance) than he does with customer service, because some people are better at using finesse and he doesn't want his clients or tenants to feel like a number in a checklist. Sometimes people need to be heard.

Then he told me what one of his customer service processes looks like. For certain situations he wants his people to say something like, "The purpose of this call is to gather all the facts, then I'll take what I've learned and work on solving your problem. Please tell me in your words what happened." Even if the solution is obvious, he instructs his people to hear the whole story. Then they can use their judgment about what to do next within certain guidelines.

When dealing with people, you can't reduce your SOP to an algorithm or a script. You have to dance with them. Let's say you're developing an SOP for your sales team, and in their initial conversation with a prospect you want them to gauge the prospect's level of interest. You can't just tell them to ask, "On a scale of 1–10, how interested are you?" Even if you could, one person's six might be another's nine. So the answers wouldn't be of much use.

What you can do is say something like this in your SOP:

Before a prospect is moved to the next stage in the sales pipeline, we want to know:

- *their budget*
- *their timeline for purchase*
- *the key players in the buying decision*

It may take more than one conversation before they are ready to share this information—and their eagerness (or lack) to share can be an indication of their interest.

Record the results of your conversation in the CRM and always try to set an appointment for the next conversation in the calendar.

If they are not willing to commit to a date for that conversation, schedule a time when you will follow up and ask for permission to follow up in that time frame. For example, "I'll check back in about three weeks. Would that be OK?" Then be sure to put an actual date/time for the follow-up, three weeks in the future.

This allows the person to dance and use their judgment, but still specifies what the output should look like. In this case, the output would be:

- details of the conversation in the CRM (which should include some facts and some judgment)
- moving the prospect to the next stage only if all the information was given
- a follow-up date in the calendar

A dance SOP means you can't describe the actual steps involved, but you should be able to specify what the output looks like. This works well when you have a dance partner. But what if you have no partner?

Documenting a Creation SOP

With this type of transformation, you can't entirely predict what the output will look like. But all creative acts have some constraints and these should be defined. Constraints can be something as narrow as the rules around making a haiku or as broad as the laws of physics. Emma Coats used to work at Pixar—a very creative place. She wrote what she called the 22 story rules. (She later said she should have called them guidelines.) Here's number 4, a great way to constrain a certain type of story creation:

Once upon a time there was __. Every day, __. One day __. Because of that, __ Because of that, __. Until finally __.[10]

A creation SOP is similar to a design brief that might be given to a graphic artist. The constraints in the brief limit the work to using certain colors and fonts and to evoking a certain mood. Then the brief would specify the size and format of the final result.

Often when documenting the transformation step, you find that what you thought was one process is really two or more. For example, take the process of handling an order. The basic flow is this: The trigger is a customer placing an order. The input is the details. The transformation is what someone does to make sure the customer's order is fulfilled properly. And the output is the handoff to the fulfillment and invoicing systems.

However, when you start to define this step by step, you might see that an order is handled differently if it comes in via email than if it comes in via phone, and different again if it arrives in person. You might need to document more systems than you thought.

Breaking down systems to their most granular level makes it easier to train others to produce at least some of the output. You may also be able to see that software can automate parts of the process that you didn't realize before.

---

[10] Michael Cavna, "PIXAR TIPS: 'Brave' artist Emma Coats shares her storytelling wit and wisdom on Twitter (#Follow-Her)," Washington Post, June 25, 2012, https://www.washing-tonpost.com/blogs/comic-riffs/post/pixar-tips-brave-artist-emma-coats-shares-her-storytelling-wit-and-wisdom-on-twitter%20followher/2012/06/25/gJQADaxd2V_blog.html.

> ### ☛ CEO TIME: Which type of SOPs do you need?
>
> Even if you're not the one documenting the systems, it might be useful for you to determine which ones fall into which category. Start with a list of the SOPs you know need to be documented soon and designate which ones are recipes, which are dances, and which are creations.
>
> Then assign someone to create them.

Output

This is the result or end state you're trying to achieve. It marks the conclusion of a run of the system. It should include relevant descriptions of quality, quantity, or other ways to know when the output is satisfactory.

One of the appeals of an org chart is how visual it is. In a similar way, if you like, you can visualize an output with a box. The box is a simple table:

System name	The name of the system or function that produces the output. **Example: Shoemaking**
Output	The description of the output. **Example: Pairs of finished shoes**

Remember all those output attributes we looked at in chapter 4? That's what you can put in additional rows if they're applicable. Things like quality metrics, numerical output, certification requirements and the like. Here's one for a fictional supervisor of a janitorial company.

System name	Supervising a nighttime janitorial shift
Output	Clean rooms produced by the janitors/room assignments/cover for no-shows
Input	The supervisor needs a job schedule and room keys or access codes
Capacity	1 supervisor should be able to oversee five janitors cleaning twelve rooms each
Cost	The cost of a supervisor is approximately xxx per room

MATURITY MODEL FOR SYSTEMS

It turns out that there's a way to score the maturity of your systems. This concept was developed in the 1980s by the Department of Defense and Carnegie Mellon University to improve the system of software development. They called it the Capability Maturity Model (CMM). I've adapted it to apply to any system in a company, not just software systems, to include five levels of system maturity.

Level 1: Work gets done

Focus on achievement

It may be behind schedule and over budget, but it gets done. Results depend on effort (often heroic) by key people.

- Goals may not exist or be very vague.

- An individual's definition of success is often "my boss is happy" or something else that's not measurable or predictable.

Level 2: Work is repeatable

Focus on repeatability of results

We can replicate results when the projects or goals are similar. This requires some metrics but most measurements are lagging indicators.

- Goals/success indicators come after the fact.

Level 3: Work is standardized, documented, and therefore trainable

Focus on standardization of process

We have a documented process for standard operating procedures.

- This is robust enough to train others.

Level 4: Work is managed in process

Focus on metrics/management

We are measuring leading indicators so results can be predicted while in process and problems corrected before the job is done, rather than fixed after the fact.

> **Level 5: Work is optimized**
> Focus on optimization
> This means that:
> - Work is aligned with the company strategy (effective, not just efficient).
> - The process is deliberately (often continually) reviewed and improved.

Not every system in your company needs to be at level 5. But the more systems that are level 3 or above, the more scalable your company is and the less dependent it will be on finding people with the exact range of skills and experience you need to grow. Let's look at how things change as your company scales.

CHAPTER 10

HOW SYSTEMS CHANGE AS YOUR COMPANY SCALES

YOU SHOULD PLAN on revising your systems at every new stage of your company's growth. It's like parenting: things that worked with a toddler don't work with a tween, and change again when your child becomes a teenager. What's different about a company is (unlike children) they don't have to grow and sometimes even go backward. Plus, you don't have to put them through college.

THE ONE-MAN BAND AND THE ORCHESTRA

Imagine a one-man band. All the music is played by the same person. Now imagine an orchestra playing the exact same tune. The musicians in the orchestra don't all play the same notes. Some play the melody and some the harmony. In fact, none of them plays all the notes like the one-man band does. But the sound of the orchestra is richer. Each musician's expertise is deeper but narrower—if the trumpeter got sick, it's unlikely that the violinist could fill in for them. And we've already talked about the role of the conductor who plays no music at all.

Yet, if the one-man band and the orchestra played the same tune, you'd recognize it as the same piece of music. How does that apply to your business? It means that all the basic outputs (the core notes of a tune in this analogy) must be produced for any company of any size. Those basic outputs for a company are:

- Serving customers: making something customers want to buy.
- Selling: finding those customers and selling to them.
- Supporting: doing all the back-office work that keeps the production and sales happening (e.g., finance, HR, facilities).
- Scaling: increasing the capacity to produce and sell.

How do the systems that produce these outputs for the one-man band end up as an orchestra (metaphorically speaking)? Too often in a business it happens "organically." That's a code word for it just grows without much of a plan. This can work to some extent, but it runs into problems. The biggest one is not being able to find or make proper use of good people, because without specifying the required outputs you aren't able to train people or even define what outputs you expect them to produce. You're at the mercy of who shows up and what shadow outputs they can figure out they need to do.

But there is another way. If you organize the outputs your company needs to produce and the systems that produce them, then you can scale them as the company grows. Systems typically scale by either duplicating or bifurcating. Let's look at each in detail.

Imagine a system to make cakes for a bakery. It looks like this:

MAKE CAKES

- Trigger: an inventory level at a certain point, a large order from a customer OR a holiday. (Note that this system has multiple triggers. You'd instruct someone to check all three at the start of a shift to determine how many cakes to prepare.)
- Input: ingredients and free time on the equipment (mixer, oven, etc.).
- Transformation: follow the recipe.
- Output: beautiful cakes for the display case.

There's a certain number of cakes that can be produced. What if we need more cakes?

HOW TO DUPLICATE SYSTEMS

One way to get more cakes is to have two crews make cakes at the same time. This is duplicating the cake system. Duplication makes sense for many systems. If your law firm needs to handle more cases, hire more lawyers. If your plumbing company needs to serve more customers, hire a new crew and put more trucks on the road doing the same thing. Many factories add a second or third shift that produces the same outputs at a different time of day.

When the input to a production system is a sale, you might find that your existing sales team can make enough sales to keep multiple crews busy. So you duplicate the production system. That's a win.

There are some real benefits to duplication:

- More output
- Crews work independent of each other
- Crews work autonomously

The downside to duplication is that it can require more capital outlay to provide equipment or capacity. You'll need trucks in the example of the plumber and attorneys for the law firm. You need enough of the system's input to justify spending the money on that extra capacity. With the bakery, you could duplicate the amount of ingredients pretty easily. But what about equipment? If you don't have enough ovens to run two crews at the same time and don't want to add more shifts, you'll have to do something else.

HOW TO BIFURCATE SYSTEMS

Another option is to bifurcate your system. That means splitting it into subsystems, where the output of one is the input of the next. We'll make baking the cakes a separate system from decorating them. This has the advantage that different people with different skills can be operating each system at the same time.

BAKE CAKES

- Trigger: an inventory level at a certain point, a large order from a customer OR a holiday.
- Input: ingredients and equipment (mixer, oven, etc.).
- Transformation: follow the recipe until the cakes are out of the oven.
- Output: cakes with no icing or decoration.

DECORATE CAKES

- Trigger: a cake from the baking system.
- Input: ingredients and equipment.
- Transformation: decorate according to the design.
- Output: beautiful cakes for the display case.

This is actually what your grandmother does when she asks you to wash and chop the vegetables while she braises the meat.

These are the main benefits to bifurcation:

- More output (if you have different people doing each subsystem at the same time).
- Lower labor costs (if some of the subsystems can be done by people with lower salaries and less training).
- More places to improve quality.

That last one is not so obvious. Ideally you want systems that prevent problems rather than fix them. By having more subsystems, quality checks can get built into your process earlier and problems are prevented more effectively than by only doing inspections at the end.

This bifurcation is the difference between the one-man band and the orchestra. No individual in the orchestra plays all the notes. But each plays their part with much more skill.

The decision of whether to bifurcate or duplicate depends on the resources you need, the capacity of each resource, and the expected throughput. Duplication usually requires more resources. In our cake example, you'd need more ovens or more people to run a second shift. If you don't have enough sales to warrant another shift, then bifurcation might be the better option. You'd just need someone with the skill of baking and another with the skill of decorating, and they could work simultaneously.

☛ CEO TIME: Give away one of your outputs

Write down one of the outputs you're constantly producing. Then answer this question: "What's keeping me from giving responsibility for it away to someone else?"

The reason usually is either that you're nervous about giving it away, or you don't have anyone who can do it as well as you.

Here's a tip. Those are both the same reasons. If you had someone who could do it as well as you, you wouldn't be nervous about giving it away. So, what can you do about it?

First of all, don't start thinking about people. Start thinking about the output itself and what it takes to produce that output. Write down the skills required.

Next, see if you have someone (or can hire someone) who can be trained to produce that output as well (or better) than you.

If that's not feasible, it's often because the output is produced by a series of subsystems. Possibly someone else can do some of them even if you need to do a few yourself. But if you don't see the subsystems as separate, you won't feel comfortable giving any of the responsibility away.

To use our cake example, baking the cake is simpler than decorating it. But if a master cake maker doesn't see that they are separate systems, they'll have a hard time giving up the job of baking because they can't find someone who's good at decorating. The cake example is a bit simplistic, but most tasks that require skill or judgment are actually composed of subtasks, some of which are much simpler.

Now think about how you can break your output down into its component parts and see if you can't give away responsibility for some of them.

Now that you're bifurcating and duplicating, things can get complicated. The number of systems and subsystems can easily outgrow the ability of you and your people to keep everything in their heads. So you need to get it down on paper (and by paper I mean electrons).

CHAPTER 11

HOW TO DOCUMENT YOUR WHOLE COMPANY

WE'VE SEEN HOW to document a single system. But after bifurcation and duplication, even a small company may have an overwhelming number of systems. You might be asking how do you document them all? The same way you eat an elephant: one bite at a time. Seriously. If you try to write down (or even imagine) how all the procedures work in your entire company, it will be overwhelming. And it's just as effective to start with the single piece you need now and add on as you go—as long as the SOPs are stored on the right platform.

Start somewhere and do it a piece at a time till you need another piece, then rinse and repeat.

When I first did this for my company, I began by documenting was how to back up the computer. This was before the days of doing it in the cloud which made it relatively complex. So I created a Word document and wrote down how to do it step-by-step. Then others could do it when I wasn't there.

Here are the steps I use with clients to document their companies:

- **Step 1.** Pick a platform where you'll store this information.
- **Step 2.** Pick a system to start with.
- **Step 3.** Get a rough first draft.
- **Step 4.** Refine that draft.
- **Step 5.** Make people use it.

Repeat steps 2–5 with a different process.
Let's get into the details.

PICK A PLATFORM

The platform is the place you'll store this documentation. It needs these characteristics:

- Easily accessible to everyone.

- A good search function.
- Able to handle text, video, images, PDFs, and any other media you might use.
- Dead simple to edit.
- **There must be only one live copy.** If previous versions need to be accessible, they should be a little hard to find, and impossible to mistake for the current version.

I strongly suggest you keep everything in a single place. If you start to organize all this information in different documents for different departments or functions, it will quickly become harder for people to find what they need and they'll stop using the documents all together. For example, suppose you segregate by department. Should the payroll system be documented under finance because there's money involved, or HR because there are employees involved? If it's all in one place where you can search, you won't have to worry about where to put it.

The obvious exception is to keep sensitive employee files, passwords, and certain financial information in separate places so they can have better security. But those are not the kinds of documents I'm talking about here.

What platform to use?

Short answer: I suggest most people use Notion (Notion.so) as your repository/database and ScreenPal (screenpal.com) to video your screen.

Long answer: These may be obsolete when you read this. I'm always hesitant to recommend software in a book because it changes so fast. When I first did this for my company, I used a single Word document stored on a computer in the office because there was no cloud. It didn't meet all the criteria above, but it was easy to search and edit.

Keep it simple. As I write this (2023) there are other platforms similar to Notion (ClickUp, Confluence, Wrike, etc.). I haven't explored them extensively. Some have a steeper learning curve and are more powerful than others. Some, including Notion, can be configured to do amazing things by manipulating data, documents, and workflow. I suggest you stay away from that level of complexity unless you need it, in which case you should treat it as a custom software project and engage a consultant who specializes in your platform of choice. Yes, I know these are promoted as "no-code" platforms but they still can be complex.

For recording video, use your phone to show manipulation of physical objects. Buy a cheap mic to get better sound, because good sound is surprisingly important for useful videos. For screen-capture video I use ScreenPal, but Loom is also popular—both allow you to record what's happening on your screen, your voice as you narrate it, as well as record your webcam. I also record Zoom calls with screen sharing. Whatever you use, if it fits the criteria above you'll be fine.

☞ CEO TIME: Pick a platform

Do you feel comfortable picking a platform to hold your company's information? If so, pick one that fits the criteria above.

If not, find someone who's more familiar with technology than you. Give them this section of the book to read and ask them to pick one that fits the criteria.

In either case, get some input from others in your company. But don't let this decision drag out too long. It's better to get started on some platform than try to find the "perfect" one. It doesn't exist.

PICK A SYSTEM TO START WITH

What system should you document first? I have three answers. Pick the one that suits your situation best.

1. If you have a system that's giving you problems, or one you'll need to train someone on right away, start there.

2. If you just want to get your feet wet on how to do this, start with accounts receivable or accounts payable. Why? These systems are already working—or you'd be out of business—and the inputs and outputs are concrete and measurable.

3. Once you feel confident in your ability to document a system, one of the most important systems to document is sales: how you get customers. But it's often one of the most chaotic. Marketing and sales may be

jumbled up. Different salespeople may be handling sales in very different ways. There may be no CRM or no standard recording of a prospect's journey through the process. This is what makes it hard, and also very valuable to systemize. See the section on sales in chapter 12 for more details on the sales system.

GET A ROUGH FIRST DRAFT

Have the person who does the work record what they're doing and talk through what they're doing as they do it. If they're doing something with a physical object, record it on a phone. If they're doing something on a computer, use screen-capture software. Then have the recording transcribed and you've got a first draft.

You want to document the work as it is actually being done. Not how it should be done—or worse, how someone who doesn't know thinks it's being done. You can always improve it later. But for now just get it down as it is. It's not critical that your videos have great production values, just that they're clear enough for someone else to follow. These processes will be changed and improved as people find new ways of doing things, but it's important to get started. Indeed, this is definitely a time to apply the saying "Don't let the perfect become the enemy of the good."

Then document the parts of the system.

- **System name:** Something clear in normal language.
- **Metadata:** Include the date and name of the person doing the write-up (or any revisions) and a brief

description of the purpose of this system or where it fits into the rest of the company.

- **Trigger:** What sets it off? When should someone do it?

- **Input:** What tools, equipment, data, parts, etc. do people need before they begin?

- **Transformation instructions:** Step-by-step instructions. The written instructions come from the transcription of the video and the document should link to (or include) the video file.

- **Output and end result:** What results indicate this system is complete?

You may find that what you thought was a single system is really composed of a number of subsystems. When an output or a result is handed off to someone else for them to do something to it, it makes sense to document the whole process as different subsystems with the output of one being the input of the next. This makes it easy to tell when someone is finished with their piece and someone else has begun theirs.

How to handle exceptions

Very rarely does a system handle 100% of every input the exact same way. Document for the most common use case and make a note about the exceptional situations. Let me tell you a story from the dark past, when phones were tethered to a wall in a permanent location and phone numbers were printed in a big book on dead tree fiber.

Sara and Chris were co-owners of a company that made small, local phone directories. They printed phone books for several local towns around their offices. These were given free to every home and business, and were paid for by business customers who purchased ads in the pages of these books printed on yellow paper.

When I started working with them, I noticed that they had a bookkeeper, but the two of them spent time every month sending out invoices to their customers. They had hundreds of customers. Why couldn't the bookkeeper do this? I asked. It would never work, they said. Why? I asked. The answer was they had often given out special deals and discounts to various customers in order to make the sale. And the details of those arrangements lived in the heads of Sara or Chris depending on who sold to that customer.

There are two lessons here. First, when we dug into it, we found most customers didn't have a special deal. About 85% were standard situations—priced based on the size of the ad and how many books they were in. It's very common for people to exaggerate how many special cases there are. While the remaining 15% of sales is not that many, it can feel like a lot. If that's the case for you, explain in your instructions how to handle exceptions, even if the way to handle them is to send them off to someone else.

The second lesson is that anything you can remember can be written down and taught to someone else. Those are the special cases. Once Sara and Chris wrote down which deals they gave to which customers, it was easy to include those deals (or a note about where to find them) in the instructions for the bookkeeper.

Finally the only input needed from Sara or Chris was a note to the bookkeeper when setting up a new customer about what kind of deal they had made or when a deal had changed. Setting up a new account is a separate system, and those instructions went there.

REFINE THE DRAFT

This step is easy. Give the draft to someone and have them follow it step-by-step. It's best if that person is not the person who created the draft, but in a pinch they can do it. You'll find stuff that's missing or needs to be clarified. Fix it. Now you've got a usable document.

MAKE PEOPLE USE IT

This may be the hardest step in the process. But it gets easier. It's a cultural shift to look to a document rather than ask a person when you need to know how something is done. However, like when dealing with any cultural shift, explain the reasoning behind it, then be consistent and firm.

Whenever someone asks a question about how to do something, you must say, "Have you looked it up in the documentation?" Look it up with them if you have to. You'll find that the documentation either answers their question or it doesn't. If it doesn't, change the documentation till it does.

You'll also use the documents with people new to the company or new to the task you're asking them to do. It has now become your training document.

REPEAT

Now that you've got one system down, do another and then another.

> ### ☞ CEO TIME: Make a task map
>
> As you document the SOPs and systems that produce your outputs, you may find it useful to develop a master list. This idea came from Peter Lohmann, who I've mentioned before. He calls it a task map. Regardless of what you call it, it's simply a table with four columns. This can be done in Notion (if that's your chosen platform) or any spreadsheet program.
>
> - The first column lists systems (or SOPs) by name. Each one has its own row.
>
> - The second column is the trigger that kicks it off (or for time-based systems, the frequency with which it needs to be done).
>
> - The third column is the person or team assigned to run the system.
>
> - The fourth column is a link to the documentation of how to do the task and produce the required output.
>
> It's useful if you can sort and filter within each column. That way you can see all the weekly tasks, or all the systems assigned to a certain team. It will also give you an idea of which SOPs have not been documented yet.
>
> | SOP or System Name | Trigger or Frequency | Person or Team | Link to Documentation |
> |---|---|---|---|
> | | | | |
> | | | | |

CHAPTER 12

SYSTEMS INVENTORY, AKA THE SEVEN BUCKETS

IN THE PREVIOUS section I said you don't need to document your entire company all at once (if ever). That's true. The best way to document systems is to do them one at a time. But as CEO, you need a way to think about the structure of your entire company that's better than an org chart. Such a view of your company structure is critical if you want to remove yourself from the day-to-day routine and not end up losing money when you're away.

There's an exercise I use with clients called the Systems Inventory to help with this. When doing so we look at all the major systems and subsystems in the company to see which outputs are being produced in a way that's repeatable and scalable, and which ones are being done by the "grandmother in the kitchen," so to speak.

In my work as a consultant and coach I've been able to see the workings of hundreds of companies of many sizes and in many industries. Those companies have thousands of outputs. Of course, there are many differences in companies, but when viewed through the lens of Output Thinking there are also a lot of similarities. The similarities are the key to how the Systems Inventory works.

I've found it useful to group the outputs into what I call buckets, as a way to view the configuration of your entire company. I use the term "buckets" because that focuses on the result, not the work that's being done. If you were starting the company as a one-man band, you'd be filling all the buckets yourself. But as the company develops into an orchestra, I've found the systems that produce the outputs subdivide in predictable ways.

This section is sort of a DIY Systems Inventory. I'll share how the major systems typically break into the first level of subsystems. I'll ask you some of the questions I ask when doing an inventory with one of my clients and share what I'm looking for. The output of the inventory is a list of how all the major systems and subsystems in the company are working to achieve the owner's goals: which ones are fine (at least for now), which ones need improvement, and which are in crisis.

Because I don't know your company specifically, I'm going to lay out the typical systems, subsystems, and outputs that come from a compilation of companies I've worked with. As with any generic approach to companies, you'll need to adapt it to your situation. You'll likely have even more subsystems than I'm mentioning, and some of the ones I'll talk about may not apply.

My goal is that you can use this information to get the perfect mix of subsystems into your company and use your CEO Time to make your business more robust. This will give you the power to remove yourself from day-to-day operations, knowing that the company doesn't depend on your continued presence.

WHAT ARE THE SEVEN BUCKETS?

They are the only reasons to spend money or effort or to hire people. We've seen these before when we talked about the one-man band, but I want to go into more depth here. These are the outputs a company must produce to survive and ultimately thrive:

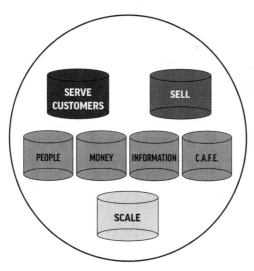

- **Serving customers:** making something customers want to buy.
- **Selling:** finding those customers and selling to them.

- **Supporting:** doing all the back-office work that keeps the serving and the selling happening (finance, HR, facilities, and the like).

  ○ The support outputs fall into four buckets: **People, Money, Information**, and **C.A.F.E.**

- **Scaling:** increasing the capacity to produce and sell.

Before we get into the details of how the buckets subdivide, here's an exercise about how to use this section of the book.

☞ CEO TIME: Make your company robust

You can view this entire section of the book as a CEO Time activity. As you read through it, keep your CEO Notebook handy. Consider how the subsystems I'm describing work in your company.

Is there a system that should be subdivided so some work can be done by a person with less training and everyone can play at the top of their game?

Is there a person who's being held accountable for each of the outputs, and are the outputs being measured with the right metrics or KPIs?

Is each system well documented?

The answers to these key questions will make your company more robust. I define a robust company as one where:

- The outputs are well defined.
- Most have at least one metric or KPI associated with them to track the quantity or quality of that output.

- There's a person accountable for achieving that metric.
- The systems used to produce outputs are well documented.
- Subsystems are broken out so everyone plays at the top of their game.

As you go through these buckets, jot down some things you can do to improve the robustness of your company and make it more ready to scale. You'll have a lot to think about here.

THE SELLING BUCKET

Your sales system fills the bucket with customers who make a purchase (or are committed to purchase). The two major subdivisions are marketing—the output of which is leads—and closing, which takes leads as the input and produces paying customers as the output. For a simple brick and mortar retailer, the marketing could be signage outside the store, attractive window displays, and advertisements. The closing happens over the counter at the cash register. For complex sales to large organizations, the sales system is more complicated with multiple marketing channels and closing systems that include product demos, engineering evaluations, and proposals or quotes.

When doing a Systems Inventory for a business, I'm looking to see what systems are in place for marketing and closing deals, and how robust they are. A robust sales system starts with answers to these three questions:

1. **Who are your customers?** No company sells to everyone in the world. Knowing who your customers are narrows your sales to people who share demographic, psychographic, or geographic characteristics.

2. **Why do they buy?** People buy because they want to solve a problem, eliminate a pain, or acquire some gain. If you know the language they use to describe their problem, pain, or gain, that language can become your marketing message.

3. **How do they make their buying decisions?** Knowing their process allows you to tailor your sales process to their buying process. You'll use marketing channels that you know are relevant to them. You'll follow up in ways that fit their buying process.

Outputs for the sales system

When designing a sales system, your design should include:

- **Personas:** A written document answering the questions above. You need one for each market you serve.

- **Marketing plan:** A description of which marketing channels you'll use, which messages you'll send, and what calls to action you hope to provoke.

- **Sales pipeline:** A description of the stages a buyer goes through. These are captured in CRM software, which also records the instances of each person going through your sales pipeline.

I'm looking to see if these are written documents, if they are up-to-date, and if they are used to inform the day-to-day work of the sales and marketing teams.

Sales management

My experience with systems inventories has shown me that the sales management subsystems are typically among the weakest systems in the company. Perhaps that is because the outputs of sales people are so visible: if they are producing then there doesn't seem to be a need to manage them. But this leads to sales people working intuitively, not systematically, so sales are not done consistently. Even more dangerous than inconsistency is that this can mean the relationships with leads, prospects, and even customers are not owned by the company. Too often, unless a sale has been made, the company doesn't even have contact information for prospects—that lives in the sales people's heads or their phones.

When the sales system and sales people are well managed, both the company and the sales people make more money. Your sales system should be designed so that every time the sales people make more money, the company does too. With a well-designed sales system it's not unheard of for a sales person to be the highest paid person in the company. If you are the owner, don't let your ego get in the way of this. After all, you own the company that they are making more valuable.

Here are the outputs you can expect from the sales management subsystem. If the company is large enough, the first four are typically produced by a sales VP or a CRO (Chief Revenue Officer) and the last three by a sales manager. But regardless of the size of the company, all of these outputs are beneficial and should be produced by someone:

- budgets for marketing and sales
- compensation plans
- division of territories and assignment of leads
- analysis of sales metrics
- sales training
- assigning sales quotas
- assistance and coaching to help salespeople meet quotas

Sales metrics

Sales metrics vary based on how your customer buys, but they typically include:

- revenue (perhaps broken out by product line)
- cost of leads broken out for each marketing channel
- conversion ratios from one stage of the buyer's journey to the next
- reasons for lost sales (used to improve product features or marketing messages)
- customer acquisition cost (CAC) for the entire system

THE SERVING BUCKET

The serving bucket (often called production) is filled with your offering to the market: products or services customers want to buy. It's how you serve customers. In job shops or make-to-order manufacturers, this system starts when a customer places an order. Service companies operate this way too. Other companies must make something ahead of a sale so there's something on the shelf for customers to buy. For them the serving system starts with a projection of what customers are expected to buy.

This is the bucket that varies most by industry. The serving system is typically where most employees work. It also often has the most subsystems, as different parts of what you sell are made by different people and handed off to others as the input to their subsystem. There can be as many as five major subsystems in this bucket, as shown in the picture above. The offering has to be designed, and raw materials and inventory have to be procured and assembled into the actual product. Then it needs to be delivered and sometimes installed at the customer's site, with any issues or problems solved by customer support.

Note that not all of these subsystems are needed by every company. For example, accountants don't get to design the tax forms on which their output is delivered. If your offering is a service, your "raw material" is people to provide that service and "procurement" is hiring. We'll cover that in a bit.

Here are the main outputs for these subsystems:

- Design produces an offering that looks, feels, and works as expected (or better).

- Procurement results in getting the raw materials, parts, and inventory at the right time and the right price.

- Assembly combines your design and raw materials into something to sell.

- Delivery produces a functional product installed at your customer's site.

- Customer support solves any problems your customers have with the product or service.

Questions I ask about the Systems for Serving Customers

Here are some questions I ask when examining the production systems in a company:

- Which of the above subsystems apply to producing your product or service?

- Are the handoffs between subsystems done properly?

- Is information handed off as well as physical material?

- How are instances of production documented as they proceed?

- Do you have redundant suppliers of key components?

Don't make procurement decisions on price alone. My video company depended on UPS to deliver our products to our customers. We also did a small amount of business with FedEx. This became important when UPS went on strike in 1997 and FedEx, knowing the situation was temporary, wouldn't take any new business if you didn't already have an account with them. Fortunately, we did.

Management

Management can provide these outputs to support employees who serve customers:

- Workflow design and scheduling. (This is often ignored for knowledge workers, but it can make them much more efficient.)
- Team leaders keep their people productive with tools, training, and the like.
- Level 2 managers allocate resources to keep people productive.

Metrics

- The ultimate metric of serving customers is COGs: cost of goods sold on your income statement.
  - If you sell a service, the salary costs of those who produce that service should be broken out into COGs (though it often isn't).
- You also want to measure levels of inventory and work in progress, so you don't invest too much money in products you aren't ready to sell, nor too little that you lose sales.
- Schedule snafus and backlogs should be measured (sometimes daily).

☛ CEO TIME: Technology as the product

This is not an output of your current production systems but something you should be considering for the future.

We usually think of technology as a tool to help us do our work faster and more accurately. Bookkeeping was done long before computers, for example, just not as well. But technology is also changing the value people want to pay for. If you aren't looking for ways to incorporate technological changes into your offering, you can get blindsided.

Here are some examples:

Looked at from the perspective of the value it provides to customers, Uber is not a technology company—it's a taxi service. Taxis have been providing temporary transportation since before there were automobiles. As technology evolved with smartphones and GPS, a new way to package that value became possible. Taxi companies could have adopted something like this, but they weren't looking at technology. They got blindsided.

Domino's uses technology to change how pizzas are purchased and from 2010 to 2018 their stock grew faster than Amazon's, Apple's, or Google's.

No one is buying technology from either of these companies, but integrating technology into the product or delivery buckets has been a game changer. Look at the changes in the music and journalism industries for other examples.

Do you have anyone on your team looking at how to incorporate technology into transformative ways of providing value to your customers?

THE SUPPORTING BUCKETS

In order to keep the selling and production going, there are many support outputs that need to be produced. These are generally similar in all companies, and they can be grouped into the four buckets shown above. As your company grows, it's important to remember that the purpose of all these outputs is to support production and sales. This attitude of service will help curtail the tendency of these parts of your company to become fiefdoms. There are a lot of subsystems in these buckets, but many of them do not require full-time work, especially in smaller companies.

SUPPORT: PEOPLE

The People bucket is filled by having the right people in the right positions doing good work. It gets filled by hiring, HR, and management. Let's look at these subsystems in detail.

Hiring

Outputs that result in good hires start with good job descriptions, then include repeatable processes for recruiting, selecting, and onboarding employees. In most SMB firms, hiring is done by managers—usually not team leaders but higher-level managers. I recommend managers devote some time every month to this work, to develop relationships with sources of good employees even when they don't have openings.

HR functions

In large companies, the hiring functions as well as several others are grouped under a department called human resources (HR). It's usually not feasible for SMB companies to have full-sized HR departments, but all the outputs that an HR department would produce are still required. They often are done by various managers. Here's how they break down:

Compliance

The output here is that processes for hiring, promoting, disciplining, and terminating employees are compliant with all relevant laws and regulations. I strongly suggest that as soon as you get ready to hire your first employee, you develop a relationship with an HR attorney or consultant to help you design systems that are compliant and will help avoid lawsuits in this area. You can continue to rely on an outside person for this until it makes sense to bring someone in house full-time.

Benefits

The output of the benefits systems is that you provide your workers with benefits that encourage them to keep working for you. What benefits to offer is decided at the top of the company, but the sourcing of benefit vendors, if not done by an HR professional, can be done by a good administrative person. Benefits like time-off and vacations are usually administered by the payroll department with input from team leaders regarding scheduling.

Employee relations

The outputs here are a way to handle disputes between employees or employees and their bosses. It can involve legal issues like sexual harassment or issues like how to announce an employee is taking maternity leave. (Yes, I've seen something like this go all the way to the CEO.) The ideal output here is no drama.

Professional development

The outputs here include performance reviews (whether formal or informal), training, and preparation for promotions. Outside consultants are often brought in for some of this.

Management

The output of good management is that people are supported to do their best work and that work is aligned with the goals of the company. Top management (level 3) sets strategic direction. Middle management (level 2) allocates resources, and team leaders (level 1) help people do their best work.

I view the output of level 1 managers as being associated with the bucket of the people they are managing: sales team leaders in the sales bucket, production team leaders in the serving bucket, etc. The output of level 3 managers falls into the growth bucket, which we'll look at shortly. Level 2 managers usually produce outputs that bridge the production and finance buckets.

Culture

Culture is the unwritten rules of how people interact in a company. It's not about foosball tables or beer bashes on Friday. It's about what gets rewarded, what gets punished, and what gets tolerated. Culture happens. If you do it well, the outputs are a culture that is consciously crafted to support your people, and your company goals and values. Some visible outputs of a consciously designed culture are:

- Communications policies are in place that express which platforms people use for which purposes, so interruptions are reduced.

- The amount of risk people are allowed to take is explained in advance.

- The balance between asynchronous work and synchronous meetings is explicit, not haphazard.

Questions I ask about the People systems

Here are some questions I ask when examining the people systems in a company:

- Are your people happy and engaged? (This is usually measured by employee retention.)

- What are the next three hires you're planning to make? (I'm looking to see if hiring is planned or done in a panic.)

- Do you plan your culture consciously or let it emerge?
- Do you have access to an HR professional, or an HR attorney to be sure your systems are compliant with local laws and regulations?
- How are training and professional development handled?
- How are interviews conducted? (I'm looking to see if there is a division of labor and diversity of inputs to the hiring decision.)
- Do all job descriptions include the outputs expected from the new hire?

SUPPORT: MONEY

The outputs of good financial systems are financial projections, insight for management decisions, and never running out of cash. Many business owners find the whole topic of finance and accounting to be confusing because these disciplines use normal words (like profit), but use them in very specific ways that can seem like a foreign language. You don't have to speak that language as a business owner, but often you need a translator. There are three main subsystems here: accounting, taxes, and finance. We'll look at these separately.

Accounting
Accounting is a group of subsystems, the output of which is clean books. Except for reports, these are pretty standard outputs and they can be systemized pretty easily.

Bookkeeping

The output of bookkeeping is that all transactions are recorded correctly, and on schedule. Also, reports are run on schedule. The ability to design the bookkeeping system (chart of accounts and reports) requires different skills and training than the ability to input transactions properly. Almost any design will work for tax purposes, but for better management decisions additional customization is usually needed.

Accounts payable (AP)

The output of accounts payable is that bills are paid appropriately. "Appropriately" means in a way that maximizes cash flow and minimizes working capital. But vendor relationships should be taken into account as well. Sometimes paying faster generates better vendor loyalty, even if it might not minimize your working capital.

Accounts receivable and collections

The output of accounts receivable and collections is that you receive the money you are owed as quickly as possible. This is measured on an aging report.

Reports

The information in your books becomes the outputs of reports. There are three standard reports: the balance sheet, the income statement, and the cash flow statement. But you often need additional reports that are customized for your situation. Something I like to keep in mind is that each report answers a specific set of questions. Often when you ask different questions, you need to design different reports.

Taxes

The best output from taxes is that you pay no more than you need to but you pay taxes on time, without penalties, and that there are no surprises. Most companies outsource their taxes to an accountant who takes your bookkeeping as the input to their work. If your bookkeeping is not done well, you'll have to pay your accountant more to do their job.

Finance

Finance takes the bookkeeping as its input and produces projections and analysis as the output. These are used to make management decisions that ensure you don't run out of cash, you know how the company makes money, and you can allocate that money to accomplish your goals.

Finance is different from accounting because accounting is about the past and entirely about the money. Finance relates those numbers to the future and to analyzing things in the real world—things like which products or customers are most profitable. Finance also analyzes the cash implications of major management decisions, such as how fast to grow or when to make new hires.

Many companies use a fractional CFO before they need a full-time person in that position. CFOs also help prepare documents when a company is raising cash from loans or from investors.

Questions I ask about Money:

- Tell me how invoices are sent and bills are paid. (I'm looking for parts of these systems to be automated, use software when possible, and be outsourced. I'm also looking for a division of labor that's consistent with fraud prevention. There are times when the owner should perform some of these tasks (typically bank reconciliation), but they should not be urgent tasks.)

- How often do you review financial reports? When are they ready? (Financials should be available by the 10th of the next month. I'm looking for regular reports and consistent turnaround.)

- What custom reports are important to you? (This gives me an idea of what metrics are important.)

- How often do you meet with your tax advisor? (I'm looking to see if my clients are getting tax planning advice or just someone to fill out the forms.)

- Do you have a CFO? How often do you meet? (Smaller companies often don't need the analysis a CFO provides, but I've seen too many companies make poor decisions that could have been improved by proper analysis. I encourage clients not to wait too long to engage a CFO.)

SUPPORT: INFORMATION AND DECISIONS

When the systems in this bucket are working properly, employees can quickly and easily access all the information they need to do their jobs well. And they can trust that the information is as accurate as possible.

Companies require many kinds of information and it should be accessible to all individuals who need it. People can't play at the top of their game if information is locked inside someone's head.

Here are some types of information you'll need to consider:

Reference documents and SOPs

A wiki or some other searchable repository of these documents is the output of a good reference system. These are things that don't change very often—though they must be kept accurate. Generally, they are accessible to everyone and should be easy to search. They could include company directories, vendor information, and, of course, SOPs about how to perform tasks and produce outputs. Because search is the key method of finding these documents, there should be rules about file naming conventions and use of keywords.

Secure documents

These documents are protected and only accessible to those who need them. Personnel files, passwords, financial information, intellectual property, and certain parts of the company's plans should be protected from unauthorized access.

KPIs and dashboards

These are ways of displaying numbers that indicate progress and milestones. Some may be privileged information that should not be accessible to anyone, but most are not. I recommend that each number be assigned to a person who is responsible for its accuracy.

Information backflow

People at the front lines in a company—those dealing with customers and vendors—often get great insights. It's important to have systems for that information to flow back up the organization to people who are not in direct contact with those outside the company.

Decisions

Good decision systems ensure that recurring decisions are made consistently no matter who makes them. They provide a framework for making and evaluating decisions, whether one-off or recurring. It's also important to have systems to communicate decisions to relevant people as soon as the decisions are made.

Questions I ask about Information and Decisions

- What KPIs and metrics are routinely tracked? How up-to-date are they?

- What platform or tools do you use to write and store SOPs and reference documents?

- Are you incorporating feedback from the people who do the work to improve the documentation of your systems and your SOPs?

- How do you get feedback from your customers? (There should be a mechanism for people who deal directly with customers to feed information back to the rest of the company.)
- What decisions are routine? How are they handled?
- Is there a process for handling one-off decisions?

SUPPORT: C.A.F.E.

C.A.F.E. stands for Compliance, Administration, Facilities, and Etcetera. These aren't systems in the same way the others are, but this group of items are things that can cause problems if they aren't taken care of. Here's a list that someone should review annually:

Compliance
Is the company in compliance with all applicable laws and regulations?

Administrative support
Is there enough support so everyone plays at the top of their game?

Facilities and equipment
Does everyone have enough space, with the right tools (in good condition) to enable them to do their best work?

Legal
Do you have the legal support you need to minimize risks and provide advice? (This typically involves contracts,

company ownership of intellectual property, and risk management.)

IT support

Do you have someone (either in house or on call) who can keep your computers, network, phones, and other technology up-to-date and running? Can new employees get set up quickly? (This is a subset of Facilities and Equipment, but is so specialized and ubiquitous that it needs its own section.)

Insurance and continuity

The outputs here are the ability to continue operations and to recover from a disaster. Insurance is often used to cover the financial costs of a problem. A good insurance broker will be able to find the best policies for your company. A great one will also tell you which insurances you don't need. Be sure to consider business interruption insurance to replace lost revenue while the company recovers from an incident, and key person insurance to provide coverage for the death or disability of all key employees—and perhaps divorce of owners or partners.

There's more to disaster survival than insurance. You should also have redundancies and backups of certain systems. This certainly means making sure your data is backed up in several places. It may also mean having options for equipment that may break or supply-chain logistics that can get backed up.

Questions I ask about C.A.F.E
- At this point in the Systems Inventory I ask about each thing on the list, how confident they are it's doing OK, and when it will be reviewed next. I'm looking for a schedule and preventive maintenance.

THE SCALING BUCKET

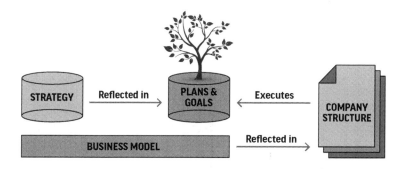

The output of scaling is greater capacity to sell and produce. It could also be greater efficiency, which results in more profit from the same amount of revenue. Many of the decisions at this level of a company are made by top management. The things that fill this bucket are the strategy, plans, and goals that help the company scale.

Strategy describes where you're going. Plans describe how you'll get there, and goals measure progress. This all must be based on the business model (how you make money), which is reflected in the company structure; and as your people produce outputs, they execute the plans resulting in growth.

Strategy

Strategy answers the questions of which markets your company will serve and how it will provide value to the customers in those markets. Many SMB companies don't answer these questions explicitly. They start out practicing law, doing plumbing, or selling real estate. The company grows organically, taking whatever business it can get. But at some point, it becomes better to specialize, so you can focus on a segment of your market that you can serve better than others.

Remember Dan, who I introduced back in chapter 2? He's the one who runs the company making parts for submarines and interplanetary spaceships. The company was started by his father as a run-of-the-mill machine shop decades before Dan took it over. One of the exercises I did with him and his team was what I call the Customer Management Matrix. It's a way to define your ideal customers and focus only on them. It turned out that Dan and his company would take work from a neighbor who needed a part of his lawn mower fixed for $50 just because they were so used to taking any work that they could. When they stopped taking customers like that, they learned that one of their best customers loved their quality, was OK with their pricing, but was not happy with how often they failed at on-time deliveries. By giving up on the lawn mower customers, they had capacity to improve their scheduling and did a better job for their ideal customers.

Plans

If a strategy sets the direction you're going, plans are how you'll get there. The output of a good planning system is a plan that will be used throughout the planning time frame to help people decide what to do and, just as importantly, what not to do. A good plan includes:

- Goals and milestones: to help you measure progress.
- Resources: commitment of money, people, and other resources to accomplish your plan.
- Accountability: to ensure people are focused on achieving the plan.
- Assumptions: what must be true for your plan to succeed. It's good to specify these when you make the plan. That way, if a plan is not working you can revisit to see if the problem is with your assumptions or your execution.

Business model

Strategy and plans are supported by your business model—which is how you make money. We could describe it as the value you capture from the transactions with your customers. Here's an example. People buy razors with disposable blades and electric razors for the same reason: they want a clean shave. But the business models of how those companies make money are very different. An electric razor company has to make a profit on each razor sold. The other company can give away the razors (or sell them at a loss) as long as they have a proprietary grasp on the ability to sell replacement blades.

Business models can change as your company grows and it's important to be aware of this. For example, a retail company can expand by adding more locations and the business model remains pretty much the same. But if it expands by selling online, or selling wholesale to other retailers, the business model has changed significantly because the cost of acquiring those new customers, as well as their lifetime value, is very different.

Company structure

By "company structure" I don't mean your org chart. I mean the way your systems are divided into subsystems. As I said before, systems scale by duplicating and bifurcating. Each of these changes requires you to hire or reassign people, train them, and perhaps purchase different equipment.

Management of your company structure results in an understanding of your current structure and the ability to predict and prepare for changes. Many times, changes to one set of systems affect others. For example, when a company is small, collections may be done by the same person who sends the invoices. But at some point, that can become a problem. You may need to implement credit checks to decide if you'll extend credit to each customer; and if so, how much. This can affect the sales system because the customer must either pass your credit check or be sold COD. Changes like this can affect the cost structure of the company, which can affect the price you need to charge for your offerings. That can affect the markets you go after.

Questions I ask about Scaling
- Is there a written strategy?
- Has the optimal amount of growth and the cost of that growth been considered?
- Are there written plans?
- Is progress against the plan reviewed regularly?
- Does everyone know how their work contributes to the success of the plan?
- How is the business model understood?
- Is the company structure optimal?
- When is it likely to change?

THE OUTPUT OF A SYSTEMS INVENTORY

The output of a Systems Inventory is an understanding of all the major systems and subsystems in the company, with a score for each, and a priority for which ones need to be worked on next. This is usually presented as a list for a discussion with the leadership team. In preparing my presentation I rate and rank the systems and subsystems.

Rating your systems
Each system or subsystem is rated by what I call DAMS:
- D = Documentation. Is it well documented?
- A = Accountability. Is there someone accountable for the outputs?

- M = Measured. Are there measurements for the outputs to track quantity, quality, or some other relevant metric?

- S = Subdivided. Is it subdivided appropriately for the current stage of the company? (This means everyone is playing at the top of their game.)

Ranking your systems

This is different from the rating. It's a guide to prioritization and deciding which systems to work on first. By looking at the owner's goals and what they want from the company, each system is either:

 **PERFECT FOR NOW**    **NEEDS IMPROVEMENT**   **IN CRISIS**

Obviously, you want to deal with the ones In Crisis first. Then work on the ones that Need Improvement. And keep an eye on the ones that are Perfect for Now. They may not be perfect as the company grows, and it can be useful to anticipate these changes. Here's an example. When a company is small, it typically doesn't have an in-house HR person. That changes at around 50 employees in the US. Knowing this and preparing for it can eliminate a lot of headaches.

CHAPTER 13

REMOVE YOURSELF FROM THE DAY-TO-DAY

BACK IN CHAPTER 1, I said you could use this book to systemize your company, scale fast, and remove yourself from the day-to-day routine. We've seen that Output Thinking is the key to systemization. When systems are repeatable and scalable, your company can scale faster and more efficiently because people play at the top of their game. Work is done by people with the lowest level of skill and training necessary. Now let's look at the last part of that promise: the ability to remove yourself from the day-to-day routine.

Demands on your time come from two places. One is the frequency of the outputs that need to be produced; this is documented in the trigger of the systems that produce those outputs. The other is urgency, which often comes from interruptions. Interruptions can be reduced or even eliminated by better systems and designing a good cadence of meetings and proper use of communication platforms.

I said earlier that outputs are more permanent than people in your company. That includes you. The company needs the outputs you're currently producing. But it doesn't need them all to be done by you. If you can use what you've learned here to separate the outputs from the people who produce them, you can enable others to produce the day-to-day outputs that the company needs. You may find people who can produce them better than you can. But even if they don't do them as well as you, they can do them well enough to serve your customers and keep your company scaling—and that frees up your time for other things.

> ## ☛ CEO TIME: Remove yourself from the daily grind
>
> Go through the list of buckets and the systems used to produce the outputs your company needs. Write down which ones depend on you. Think about the urgency or frequency of those outputs and how it puts demands on your time. Then work out which outputs you can give away so that the output is produced as well (or better) by someone else.
>
> Another way to achieve the same result is to do a time log as you go through your day, jotting down not what you're doing but what output your work is intended to produce. This is equivalent to asking *why* you're doing something, not *what* you're doing. For example, if you spend two hours a day on email, that's what you're doing. However, if

the output of your email is sales, it's a very different situation than if your output is solving customers' problems. Do your time log based on outputs and then see which ones you can give away.

By "give away" I mean more than a one-off delegation. I mean assigning responsibility and authority to produce the outputs in a way that you're confident the output will be done well without any involvement on your part.

You can download the time log template here: https://decipherpublications.com/output-thinking-extras/.

You may not have someone you can hand these outputs to immediately; if that's the case, devise a plan to train someone. You may need to grow the company so you can afford to do this without diminishing your take-home pay. But empowering others to produce the outputs that used to depend on you is how you can run a company that doesn't require your continual production of day-to-day activities.

Unlike Larry, I and many of my clients have successfully pulled ourselves out from the day-to-day workings of our companies. Some moved away, some built other companies, some have acquired other companies to start a holding company. And others kept working but they transitioned to do more of the kind of work they enjoyed.

Too many business owners plan their days by urgency. They react to which outputs are falling on their shoulders and respond to the most urgent, not necessarily the most important. Instead, I suggest you use the bucket framework to take a step back and look at the overall

structure of your company. Then use that insight to determine which outputs you want to be involved in producing or managing.

If you understand the way the buckets fill in your organization, it gives you tremendous power. You can decide which buckets you want to work on and which you
don't. Solo entrepreneurs have no choice. They've got to
fill all the buckets themselves. Admittedly at that scale,
most of the support buckets don't take a lot of time. So
they spend most of their efforts on sales and serving customers. But you have a choice. You can hire and empower
people to fill all the buckets the company needs, and only
work on the ones you want to.

What you can't do is ignore some of the buckets. The
company needs them all filled to some degree. That's
what I meant when I said earlier that the outputs are
more permanent than the people. This is your chance to
design your company in a way that serves your ultimate
goals. And speaking of your ultimate goals, we need to
talk about the eighth bucket.

THE EIGHTH BUCKET

Here's a conceptual diagram illustrating how money
flows into and out of a business. Customers pay money
and receive something they value. You spend that money
filling those seven buckets to ultimately find those customers and produce that value for them. When done at
the right scale, you spend less than customers pay and
you capture some of that value as profit: that's the eighth

bucket. You then decide how much of that profit to reinvest and how much to take out as distribution.

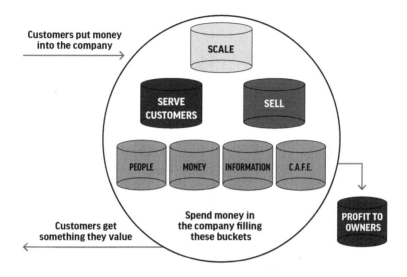

The thing about the eighth bucket that's unique is that it only fills up if you focus on the other seven. In that sense it's like happiness. Too much focus on your own happiness can actually make you less happy than if you focus on other things. Likewise in business, if you focus on your customers' passion, not yours, and if you make your company a better place for employees to work, you're more likely to have a successful company *and* get what you want too.

While the purpose of a business is to create a customer, nobody runs a company just for the customers' benefit. There's something we all want *from* our companies that keeps us motivated to grind through the fear and fight for those bits of exhilaration that being an SMB owner can bring. And yes, I know that we're in it to make a profit. Without at least the potential for profit, you don't have a business. It's a hobby perhaps, or a charity, or some other worthy endeavor, but not a business.

As the infomercial says "But wait! There's more!" Let's zoom into that eighth bucket.

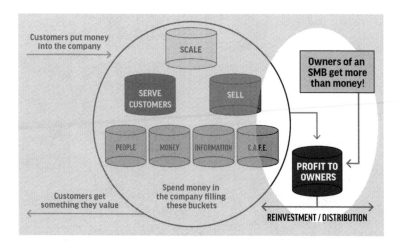

There are many other reasons to own a business in addition to profit. This, in my mind, is the best thing about the SMB world compared to the Wall Street world. Wall Street only considers financial return when it values a company. But as any SMB owner will tell you, there's a lot more than money that keeps us in the game. There's the freedom of being your own boss, the ability to make a difference for your customers and your employees, and the potential to craft a lifestyle you want. The eighth bucket is the ability of your company to provide not only profit, but all the things that inspired you to run your business in the first place.

If you don't do it excellently, don't do it at all. Because if it's not excellent it won't be profitable or fun, and if you're not in business for fun or profit, what the hell are you doing here?

—ROBERT TOWNSEND IN *UP THE ORGANIZATION*

Bob ran a small law firm. He hired me because his entire staff had walked out on him—twice. Not all at once, but he'd had 200% turnover in a very short time. After we'd been working together for a while, he told me his wife was expecting their second child. I asked him how he wanted the experience of his second child to be different from that of his first. His answer was that he didn't want to work on the weekends. He wanted to spend that time with his family. But that's all he really said about his personal life.

I'm not a therapist, but I know that our companies and our lives are interconnected. Life skills are not why clients hire me, but sometimes the topic comes up and I'm happy to share what I've learned running companies for over 40 years, having two marriages (one that works) and raising five kids. But Bob never brought it up again. And that's OK too.

We solved Bob's staff problem (by making him a better boss) and as we had our final session, I asked him what was different because of our work together. His answer surprised me. I knew about the financial and manageri-al improvements and expected him to talk about those. Instead, he didn't mention any of that. He told me the biggest changes were more time with his family, more involvement with his church, and time to work out and get in better shape. Even though in years of working together, he'd never mentioned any of that, I was happy to see that he could now use his business to provide what was really important to him.

In my decades of working with owners of privately held companies, I've found there are three things almost everyone wants from their companies: more money, more time off, and more enjoyment at work. Beyond those three, I've uncovered about two dozen things that drive people to own and run their companies—though most of them don't apply to everyone.

These are outputs of the highest level because they are what people want *from* their companies. Many planning methods start with your vision *for* your company. A typical question is, "Where do you see your company in ten years?" But if you don't specify what you want *from* your company, you might build it in a way that doesn't get you what you really want, even if you achieve your vision *for* it.

Consider two similar companies, one owned by someone who loves to travel and one by a homebody who hates any voyage beyond their local coffee shop. This would affect what kinds of customers they go after, where and how fast they want to grow their companies, and many other decisions. The truth is that those desires will affect your business decisions even at a nonconscious level. So I suggest you put those desires on the table and deal with them directly. A robust company gives you more power to achieve what you want from and for your company.

I'll leave you with one last CEO Time exercise—it's the one I use first when I start working with a client. I realize it scares some people to think about what they really want. But it's so powerful when you do it.

☛ CEO TIME: What do you want?

For this exercise, I want you to think of your business as a genie. But instead of rubbing a lamp to get your wishes, you have to go to work. Why are you working for this particular genie at this time in your life? What do you want *from* your business?

Take some time to think about that and make some notes in your CEO Notebook. They don't have to be logical—by that I mean, suppose you want to sell your company for $10 million. (That's a common number I hear, by the way.) It doesn't have to logically or actually be worth that for you to want that much. Write it down and then see if you can't use what you're learning here to make the company worth that much.

The top three things that almost everyone wants from their company are:

1. Money (now as income and in the future as equity).
2. Time (usually time away from the business).
3. Work that they love.

I'll add a fourth one that is more popular now with technology being what it is:

4. Live where you want. I did this even before the internet, using systems to run my Texas company from my home in Connecticut.

I have a worksheet available that covers about two dozen things I've collected over the years that business owners say they want. Download the worksheet template here: https://decipherpublications.com/output-thinking-extras/.

CONCLUSION

Owning and running a business is not for everyone. Thank goodness, or there'd be no one left to work for us. But for people who enjoy the rush that comes from making a sale and the exhilaration of building a team that works together to grow a company I think there's no more exciting way to earn a living and craft a life.

I wrote this book because I'm limited in the number of companies I can work with at any given time, and I wanted to share some things I've learned throughout my business career. I hope it gave you some of the insights I wish I'd had when I was starting my entrepreneurial journey—one that has been an exciting, sometimes terrifying, but an overall satisfying and very lucrative adventure. I wish the same for you.

Drop me a line and let me know how your journey is going. I'd love to hear about it. My email address is John@CEOBootCamp.com and I'd appreciate it if you'd leave a review of this book on Amazon using the QR code on the next page.

Leaving a review on Amazon is so helpful for indie authors like me, and I thank you!

ACKNOWLEDGEMENTS

It's been said that success has many parents but failure is an orphan. It's too soon to say if this book will be an orphan, but on the off chance it is not, I want to credit its many parents. First of all, my heartfelt thanks to my employees who put up with me as I was learning to be a better manager. I am indebted as well to my clients who have taught me so much through the years.

I wouldn't have become a business coach without Debra Whiddon who called me up one day and said I should look into this thing called coaching and that I'd be good at it. Until then, I'd never heard of coaching other than in sports. Nor would I have become a coach without the work of the late Thomas Leonard and those I worked with in the early days of Coach U and the International Coach Federation (now the International Coaching Federation). That list includes:

Jay Perry (special shout out to Jay who was my first coach), Laura Berman Fortgang aka LBF, Susan Klein, Jeff Raim, Sandy Vilas, Shirley Anderson, Joan Cook,

Cheryl Richardson, Madeleine Homan Blanchard, Stephen Cluney, Philip Cohen, Laura Hess, Steve Straus, Judy Feld, Cindy Reinhardt (who along with Guy Stickney (RIP) ran the best ICF conference ever, and then, when she thought she was going out in a blaze of glory, at my urging did it again the next year and surpassed herself), Bobette Reeder, Ed Shea (who did an amazing job of Imago therapy by phone), Sherry Lowry, DJ Mitsch, Rich Fettke, Christine McDougall (who gave the ICF a terrific start in Australia), Barbara Walton, Chrissy Carew, Katherine Halpin, and Marcia Reynolds (who took the reins of the ICF as President after me). My apologies to anyone I left out—it wasn't intentional.

I resisted the idea of writing a book for many years until I read *Write Helpful Books* by Rob Fitzpatrick who convinced me it was worthwhile. Thanks to him and his writing group at HelpThisBook.com for inspiring me to keep going when I might have given up. I have to mention my wonderful editor, Harriet Power, who didn't hold back from demolishing my first draft and in the process made me realize a whole lot of what I had to say wasn't even in that version. And I'm indebted to Saeah Lee Wood, Amy Reed, and the team at Otterpine for the design of the cover and the book.

In the last few years there has been an amazing (and amorphous) group of SMB owners on Twitter (now X) who are more than willing to connect online and in real life to share what they're up to and what they've learned. Meeting many of them has been inspiring, enlightening, and a whole lot of fun. My hat's off to you gentlemen and ladies.

Most of all I am grateful to my wife, Denise, who has been so supportive on my journey—she even ran my video business for the last half of its life. But most of all she's made the whole journey worthwhile.

—John Seiffer
Pittsburgh, PA 2023

ABOUT THE AUTHOR

 John Seiffer has been a se-
rial business owner since
1979. He's been coach-
ing business owners since
1994 and was part of the
team that founded the In-
ternational Coaching Fed-
eration. He became their
fourth president in 1998.
He has also been an angel investor and was president of
the Angel Investor Forum in 2012 and 2013. He turned
over the ownership of his video business in 2016 and in
2023 learned it may have outlasted the DVD-in-the-mail
division of Netflix. Ask him about it—it's a crazy story
that is beyond the scope of this book. He currently lives
in Pittsburgh, PA and continues to coach and consult
with business owners, as time permits. Follow his work
at CEOBootCamp.com.

Made in the USA
Columbia, SC
26 August 2024

41171164R20104